D1034542

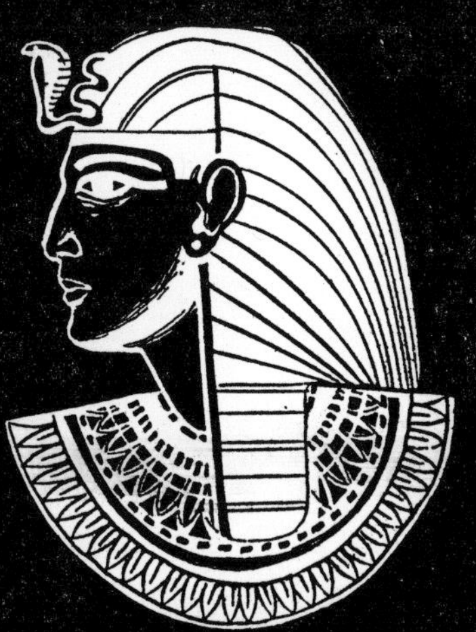

Words from the Exodus

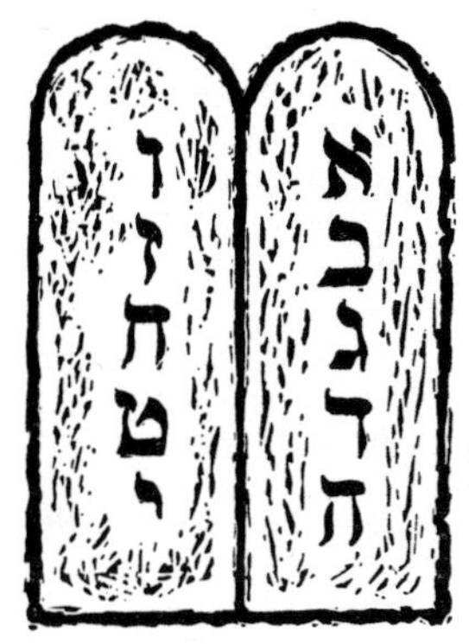


# Words from the Exodus

Isaac Asimov

*Decorations by William Barss*



1963

HOUGHTON MIFFLIN COMPANY BOSTON

The Riverside Press Cambridge

Houghton Mifflin Books

by Isaac Asimov

---

Words of Science

Realm of Numbers

Breakthroughs in Science

Realm of Measure

Words from the Myths

Realm of Algebra

Words in Genesis

Words on the Map

The Human Body

Words from the Exodus




LIBRARY OF CONGRESS CATALOG CARD NUMBER: 63-7136
PRINTED IN THE U.S.A.

# CONTENTS

*To my mother*

*ANNA RACHEL ASIMOV,*

*With love*

# PREFACE

SOME TIME AGO, I succumbed to a temptation of many years' standing and proceeded to write a book about the Bible. It was not religion itself I wanted to write about, for I am not a theologian. I wanted to write about the words in the Bible. My trade, after all, lies in words, and those of the Bible are the most influential of all in English literature. They have insinuated themselves into every cranny of our language and have grown so familiar, indeed, that we almost forget how they arose. I wanted to remind those who had forgotten of what the Bible means to the English language.

However, the Bible is such a gold mine of words and phrases that I quickly saw the story could not be confined within the covers of a reasonably sized volume. So I contented myself with but the first book of the Bible and, eventually, *Words in Genesis* (Houghton Mifflin, 1962) appeared. In that book, I had the fun of finding "God" in "giddy" and "holy" in "Halloween." The "babble" of confused languages turned out to have nothing to do with the Tower of "Babel," and the pleasure of writing about such things was great.

But then can one take up the Bible and leave it after the first book? I couldn't.

Here, therefore, is a continuation of the search for the words and phrases to which the Bible has given life and meaning; of some of the stories behind them, and some of the adventures that have befallen them. In this book, *Words from the Exodus*, I deal with the books of Exodus, Leviticus, Numbers, and Deuteronomy.

This, of course, doesn't finish the Bible either. I have the feeling then that I am not yet done. . . .

# Words from the Exodus

# 1

## Egypt

In ancient times, long before the time of the Greeks, Egypt was already the wonderland of the world. It had ancient traditions stretching back into the dim beginnings of civilization. It had tremendous monuments and temples whose origin was lost in legend.

It was a rich land of many people and of almost unfailing harvests, thanks to the annual overflow of the Nile River.

Egypt plays an important part in the earliest traditions of the Hebrew people. Abraham and Jacob, two of the three patriarchs from whom the Jews consider themselves to be descended, visited Egypt. Even in the days of these patriarchs, the description of Egypt is that of a nation already rich, cultured and powerful.*

Abraham's visit was only temporary. He went to Egypt merely to escape the effects of a famine then raging in Canaan (the region which later came to be known as the land of Israel). When the famine was over, he returned.

The story of Jacob was more complicated. Joseph, the eleventh of his twelve sons, was sold by his elder brothers into slavery and was brought down to Egypt. In Egypt his ability raised him to the heights and he became what we would now call a Prime Minister, and the power behind the throne.

Later, famine drove Jacob to send his remaining sons to Egypt to buy grain. For a while, Joseph was human enough to inflict sufferings upon them as pun-

---

* The story of the patriarchs is given in Genesis, the first book of the Bible. I discussed Genesis in my book *Words in Genesis* (Houghton Mifflin, 1962).

ishment for their mistreatment of himself. In the end, though, there was a reconciliation and the whole family was brought into Egypt to be settled there permanently.

It is with that settlement that the Book of Genesis ends.

The next four books of the Bible deal with the life of the descendants of Jacob in Egypt and of their return to their ancestral home in Canaan.

Having already discussed Genesis in my previous book, I would now like to take up these next four books — Exodus, Leviticus, Numbers, and Deuteronomy. As before, my main interest is not in theology, or in trying to interpret the teachings of the Bible, or to judge its historical accuracy. I am interested in the names and words and phrases of the Bible, and in how they have influenced our language and entered our everyday speech.

Before we take up the story, however, let's take a quick look at Egypt and its early history.

The Hebrew name for Egypt is *Mizraim* and the Arabic name, even today, is *Misr*. (Arabic is closely related to ancient Hebrew.)

The Greek name for the land was *Aigyptos*. This may have been their pronunciation of the Egyptian name of some prominent city of the land of the Nile.

This became *Aegyptus* in Latin and "Egypt" in English.

In English, "Egypt" has a soft *g*, but in Greek and Latin, the *g* was hard. The Egyptians themselves, in Roman times, adopted the Graeco-Latin name for the land and called themselves *Gyptios* (with a hard *g*). When the Arabs conquered Egypt in the seventh century A.D., they called the inhabitants by their version of that name, shifting the hard *g* to a hard *c* and pronouncing it something like "Kibt."

In English, this becomes "Copt," and to this day, the term is used for those Egyptians who speak the language and practice the religion that prevailed before the Arabs came. The Coptic language is descended from later versions of the original Egyptian language. It is written with the Greek alphabet (Greek was the language of Egyptian rulers for the thousand years from 330 B.C., to A.D. 639). It was with the help of the Coptic language that the ancient Egyptian inscriptions were worked out a century and a quarter ago.

The Egyptian religion, before the coming of the Mohammedan Arabs, was a form of Christianity. The word "Copt" is used for those Egyptians who still practice Christianity and their religious organization is the "Coptic church."

The word "Egypt" traces its way into modern speech along another route as well.

This involves a group of wandering people who, from their language, seem to have originated in India. In the ninth century, they had penetrated Persia and by the eleventh century, they were in southeastern Europe. They reached western Europe in the fifteenth century.

The wanderers were given varying names in the different languages, according to the local theory as to their place of origin. In France, for instance, they were thought, for some reason, to have come from Bohemia (part of modern Czechoslovakia). For this reason, they were called Bohemians.

These wanderers did not fit into the settled society which surrounded them but insisted on keeping their own customs. Consequently, anyone who lived a wandering life or who refused to settle down but insisted on being unconventional was called a "bohemian" by the French. The word was picked up by English-speaking people and we talk of the bohemian life of Greenwich Village in New York, for instance.

In England, the theory was that these wandering people from the East came from Egypt. They were therefore called "Egyptians" and the word was shortened to "Gypsies." This word is also used to express a wandering and unconventional nature. A desire to travel is explained sometimes by the phrase "It's the gypsy in me."

The Gypsies were experienced horse-traders, this being one of their ways of making a living. It was rare that anyone could bargain with a Gypsy over a horse and get the better of it. Naturally, a person who had dealt with Gypsies and gotten the worse of it considered himself cheated or "gypped."

And so we find we have traveled from the first of the grand civilizations, to a slang term for "cheat" by a very complicated route.

Among the ancient peoples of classical times, Egypt was already a land of mystery. Her ancient history was unknown to the Greeks. The queer picture language that covered her temples and monuments was already lost to the common people. The Egyptian priests hoarded it as a secret and sacred language so that the Greeks called the picture-writing "hieroglyphics" (hy′er-oh-glif′iks), from Greek words meaning "sacred writing."

About 280 B.C., an Egyptian priest named Manetho (man′eh-tho) decided to write an authentic history of Egypt from the temple records that were available to him. In doing so, he listed all the kings of Egypt, dividing them into families. Over a period of time, the kingship would descend from father to son, or through some other close relationship. Then a completely new family would establish itself, perhaps as a result of a civil war or a foreign conquest.

The families were called "dynasties" (die′nus-teez), from a Greek word meaning "to have power." A dynasty was the family having power over the land, in other words. There were thirty of these ruling families (some of them, especially toward the end, foreign and not Egyptian) and so one can speak of the thirty dynasties of Egypt.

Sometimes the different royal families that have held power in other countries are referred to as dynasties, but the word is most often applied to Egyptian history.

Unfortunately, Man′etho's book did not survive. The only records we have of it now are in the form of short summaries in the books of later writers in Greek and Latin. We don't know exactly how accurate the summaries are, or what their writers left out. Furthermore, after Rome became Christian, writers tried to make Manetho's material fit the details given in the Bible, and that meant more distortions.

Even so, Manetho's list of kings remained and, on the whole, it seems to be accurate. In the nineteenth century, when the hieroglyphics were finally deciphered, the inscriptions referred to kings that seemed to fit fairly well with Manetho.

The actual dates of the various dynasties are, naturally, uncertain, but I will use the information given in the Revised Third Edition of *An Encyclopedia of World History*, edited by William L. Langer (Houghton Mifflin, 1952).

According to this book, the first dynasty was established about 2900 B.C. The traditional name of the first king of this first dynasty is Menes (mee′neez) and he is supposed to be the first to have united the whole land of Egypt under a single rule. The period before Menes is referred to as "pre-dynastic Egypt" and the land was the center of considerable civilization even then.

Egypt rose to particular power under the third dynasty, which came to the throne about 2700 B.C. It was in that dynasty that the first pyramid was built by a king named Zoser. The largest pyramids were built by the kings of the fourth dynasty. The Great Pyramid itself, the largest, was built about 2500 B.C., by a king whom the Greeks called Cheops (kee′ops), but whose Egyptian name was closer to Khufu (koo′-foo).

The period of strength under the third, fourth, fifth, and sixth dynasties, from 2700 to 2200 B.C., is referred to by the name of "Old Kingdom."

After these dynasties, civil war disrupted the land. The power of the kings declined and each local district was a law to itself. A series of short-lived dynasties filled the next century.

Central authority was re-established by the eleventh dynasty in 2100 B.C., and it and the twelfth dynasty represent, together, the "Middle Kingdom." This lasted till 1788 B.C.

Another period of chaos followed and, in 1680, a group of Asian nomads took advantage of this time of weakness to invade Egypt from the east. The Egyptians called them *Hyksos* (hik′sose), which may have meant "foreign kings." (Later, the suggestion was made that it meant "shepherd kings," but this is probably wrong.) Manetho assigned the fifteenth and sixteenth dynasties to the Hyksos.

The Egyptians finally rose in revolt against the Hyksos, and in 1600 B.C. a group of Egyptian rebels set up a native government in opposition to the Asians. These rebels made up the seventeenth dynasty.

In 1580 B.C., however, the Hyksos were finally expelled by the Egyptians under the energetic leadership of Amosis (a name, pronounced ah-moh′sis, which is also spelled Ahmose, Ahmes, or Aahmes —

for there is always some argument as to the exact English letters into which to convert the Egyptian picture-writing).

Amosis was the first king of the eighteenth dynasty. From the standpoint of military power and warlike glory, the eighteenth dynasty marks the Egyptian peak. Thutmosis III (thoot-moh′sis) of that dynasty, ruling from 1501 to 1447 B.C., conquered large sections of Asian land to the northeast of Egypt. He is sometimes called the Napoleon of Egypt and is the first king in history to be called "the Great."

A later king of the dynasty was Amenophis IV (am′ih-noh′fis), who ruled from 1375 to 1358 B.C. He tried to establish the worship of the sun as the one and only god, in place of the large variety of gods of all sorts worshiped by the Egyptians. He even abandoned his name because it contained that of the god Amen and adopted the name Ikhnaton (ik-nah′tun) because it contained "Aton," the name of the sun-god.

The worship of one god is "monotheism" (from Greek words meaning "one god") while the worship of many is "polytheism" ("many gods"). Ikhnaton is sometimes called the first monotheist in history.

However, Ikhnaton's monotheism was not popular with the Egyptians, and polytheism returned to full power after Ikhnaton's death. He was followed by weak young rulers, including the famous Tutankhamen (toot′ahnk-ah′men), whose intact tomb was discovered in 1922.

The eighteenth dynasty therefore declined and the nineteenth dynasty took its place. The nineteenth and twentieth dynasties included a large number of kings named Ramses (ram′seez) or Rameses, so that the kings of the two dynasties are sometimes lumped as the "Ramessids" (ram′uh-sidz).

The most powerful of the Ramessids was Ramses II, who enjoyed a long rule from 1292 to 1225 B.C. and who fought wars in Asia. After him, the final decline set in.

During the reign of the successor of Ramses II, Merneptah (mer′nep-tah′), the whole ancient world was thrown into confusion by the invasion of barbarian peoples. The Egyptians called them the Peoples of the Sea, for they attacked Egypt from the North, across the Mediterranean. They were beaten off with difficulty, but Egypt lost its Asian territories.

The Peoples of the Sea included the Achaeans (uh′-kee′unz), the Greeks of whom Homer sang, who were apparently expanding from Greece across the islands of the Mediterranean and onto the Asia Minor coast. The Trojan War seems to have been an item in this expansion.

The attacking Achaeans seem to have driven a group of people out of either Crete or Cyprus (two large islands in the eastern Mediterranean). These people sought refuge on the coast of Canaan and were the Philistines with whom later books in the Bible are very much concerned.

The eighteenth, nineteenth, and twentieth dynasties are lumped together as the "New Kingdom" or "the Empire," and this lasted until 1090 B.C. By 1090 B.C., however, the decline was complete, and Egyptian power was over. Egypt was invaded first by Libyans from the west, then by Ethiopians from the south, and, in 671 B.C., by Assyrians from the east. After a short Egyptian revival, the Macedonians under Alexander the Great conquered the land. The last of the Macedonian monarchs was the famous Cleopatra, and in 30 B.C. she lost the land to the Romans.

How does Biblical history fit into this long pattern of rise and fall of Egyptian power?

Well, actually, the Bible does not give dates in the modern fashion for its events. Biblical scholars have therefore had to supply dates only after considerable deduction and guesswork.

Many editions of the Authorized Version* of the

* The Authorized Version is popularly called the King James Version because it was first published in the reign of King James I of England, 350 years ago. I use this version for my quotations, because the King James is the version that has made its mark on the English language. I will occasionally refer to a modern translation of the Bible, the Revised Standard Version, published in 1952.

Bible include a system of dates worked out by Archbishop James Ussher of the Anglican church in the early seventeenth century.

According to this scheme, the creation took place in 4004 B.C. and Noah's Flood in 2349 B.C., just at the end of the fifth dynasty.*

Abraham lived about two centuries after the Flood and traveled into Egypt, according to Ussher, in 2126 B.C. This would be during the chaotic times between the Old Kingdom and the Middle Kingdom. Abraham, if this date is taken as correct, could then travel as he chose through Canaan and Egypt. There would be no central authority to control him or demand passports.

Ussher's date for the selling of Joseph into slavery is 1729 B.C., while Jacob and his family followed in 1706 B.C. This, again, is during a period of Egyptian weakness, between the Middle Kingdom and the New Kingdom.

In fact, the entry of Jacob and his family, according to Ussher, is close to the date given by Langer's book for the invasion of Egypt by the Hyksos. It might almost seem that Jacob and his family came in with the Hyksos, at a time when Egypt was open to

---

* There is no mention at all, in any of the Egyptian records we have, of the Flood, or of any of the people or events described in the early books of the Bible.

the migration of Asian peoples from the east.

It might even be that the friendly Pharaoh who raised Joseph to power and welcomed Jacob (see *Words in Genesis*) was one of the early Hyksos pharaohs, who may have considered Jacob's family to be fellow Asians.

But the second book of the Bible opens after a considerable gap of time and the situation with respect to the descendants of Jacob has completely changed . . . .

# 2

## Moses

The second book of the Bible begins with the phrase "Now these are the names" or, in Hebrew, *v'elleh shemoth*. Now the Jews customarily name the early books of the Bible after the first words. For that reason, the Hebrew name for the second book is *v'elleh shemoth*, or, simply, *shemoth* ("names").

When the Bible was first translated into Greek by the Jews of Alexandria, Egypt, in 250 B.C.,* this second book was, naturally, given a Greek word as its title. Since it deals mainly with the events leading to the departure of the descendants of Jacob from Egypt, the book was named *Exodos* meaning "a going out." This became *Exodus* (ek′soh-dus) in Latin.

The Biblical use of this word has made it part of the English language. With a capital letter, the word refers particularly to the events of this book. With a small letter it can refer to any departure of a number of people.

In quoting from the book, I shall use the abbreviation "Ex." and will follow it with the number of the chapter and verse. Thus, "Ex.2:3" will mean "Exodus, chapter 2, verse 3."

Exodus begins with a quick summary of the final events in the book of Genesis. In this way, the two books are tied together.

---

* As I explained in *Words in Genesis*, the Jews, after the time of Alexander the Great, spread over a wide area of the Mediterranean world. There was a particularly large and prosperous colony in Alexandria, which was then the capital of Egypt. These Alexandrian Jews began to use Greek as their language and slowly forgot the ancestral Hebrew. In order that they might not lose touch with the Bible, they arranged to have it translated into Greek.

Ex.1:1. *Now these are the names of the children of Israel, which came into Egypt; . . .*

Jacob bore the alternate name of "Israel," and the phrase "children of Israel" refers in this case to Israel's (or Jacob's) actual children. Later in the book, and in the Bible generally, however, "children of Israel" refers to all of Jacob's descendants to any number of generations.

It does not, of course, refer only to "children." If we were to say "the children of America" we would mean the young boys and girls. The phrase "the children of Israel" includes, however, all Israelites of any age.

The names of Jacob's sons are listed and then the passage of time is indicated:

Ex.1:6. *And Joseph died, and all his brethren, and all that generation.*

Ex.1:7. *And the children of Israel were fruitful, and increased abundantly, and multiplied . . .*

Then came a crisis in the affairs of the Israelites, leading to their enslavement:

Ex.1:8. *Now there arose up a new king over Egypt, which knew not Joseph.*

Joseph, according to the story in Genesis, had ruled Egypt wisely and to the benefit of the Egyptians. Consequently, his family was well treated, if only for the sake of his memory. But now a king came to power who could disregard the memory of Joseph. This seems to mean that a new dynasty came to power.

Perhaps it was the eighteenth dynasty and the king referred to was Amesis. Then one could suppose that the new king was a native Egyptian who hated the Hyksos and the Asians that had come in with them. It would become a matter of patriotism to "know not Joseph."

The traditional date system of Ussher puts the events of the Book of Exodus between the years 1531 B.C. and 1491 B.C., or just before the reign of the great Thutmosis III, according to the chronology in Langer. This is well after the eighteenth dynasty rose to power.

Perhaps, then, the new king was the first important king of the nineteenth dynasty. That would be Seti I, who began his rule in 1313 B.C. But he was followed by Ramses II, who reigned long and victoriously, and that doesn't fit the Book of Exodus.

Traditionally, the king referred to in Ex.1:8 is Ramses II himself. He was followed by the weak king Merneptah, in whose reign there were the destructive raids of the Peoples of the Sea. That seems to make more sense.

In any case, the new king (let us say Ramses II) feared that the Israelites, being of Asian descent, might side with another invading host from Asia. This was particularly important since the Israelites lived in Goshen, which was adjacent to Egypt's Asian frontier. The decision was made, therefore, to put them to hard service and wear them out:

> Ex.1:11. *Therefore they did set over them taskmasters to afflict them with their burdens. And they built for Pharaoh treasure cities, Pithom and Raamses.*

"Pharaoh" is the traditional name for all the Egyptian kings during the Biblical period (as I explained in *Words in Genesis*).

As for Pithom (py′thom) and Raamses (ray-am′-seez), they were located east of the Nile delta, fronting the isthmus of land across which Asian nomads might invade after the fashion of the Hyksos. They were on the borders of Goshen, where the Israelites lived.

The cities were apparently not treasure cities in the sense that Pharaoh filled them with gold and silver. However, the ruins of Pithom ("pa-tum" in Egyptian, meaning "house of Tum," Tum being one of their gods) show subterranean chambers which were probably used to store grain. This, in case of a siege, would have been a treasure indeed. The Revised Standard Version, therefore, refers to the cities, more logically, as "store-cities."*

The name of the second city makes it seem logical that it was founded by a pharaoh named Ramses and named after himself. Ramses II was the most powerful of the Rammesids and filled Egypt with monuments praising himself. He is quite likely to have named a city for himself.

For these reasons, Ramses II is quite commonly called the Pharaoh of the Oppression. Moreover, because of these first verses of Exodus, "Egyptian bondage" has come to mean any kind of hard service, cruelly enforced.

Despite the enforced labor, however, the Israelites continued to multiply, and Pharaoh decided to take more direct action. He ordered that all male babies born to the Israelites be destroyed. Consequently,

---

* There have been some readers of the Bible who felt that the enslaved Israelites were set to building the pyramids. However, the pyramids were built a thousand years before the traditional time of the Book of Exodus. As a matter of fact, the pyramids are never mentioned in the Bible.

when a woman of the tribe of Levi (lee′vigh), the third of Jacob's sons, gave birth to a little boy, she hid him to save him from death, and when she could do so no longer, she took desperate measures:

> Ex.2:3. *And when she could not longer hide him, she took for him an ark of bulrushes, and daubed it with slime and with pitch, and put the child therein; and she laid it in the flags by the river's brink.*

Bulrushes are sturdy reeds that grow at the edge of a river. As a matter of fact, the bulrushes were papyrus reeds, of which writing material was made, and which gave its name, finally, to "paper" (see *Words in Genesis*).

The word "ark" recalls Noah's ark, about which I spoke in *Words in Genesis*. In both cases, the ark is a chest protecting its contents from harm. Noah's ark was a large chest housing many men and animals. This ark was a tiny one to protect an infant.

The river is the Nile. The name is from the Greek "Neilos" but nobody knows where the Greeks got the name.

As it happened, the infant was found by Pharaoh's daughter, who took pity on the crying baby, though she knew it must be an Israelite child. The baby's older sister, standing near by, offered to fetch a nurse and, of course, fetched her own mother. (The sister will appear again in the story.)

When the child grew beyond the nursing stage, the mother turned him over to Pharaoh's daughter, glad, no doubt, to feel that in the care of the princess, the youngster would be spared slavery and death. As for Pharaoh's daughter —

> Ex.2:10. . . . *he became her son. And she called his name Moses: and she said, Because I drew him out of the water.*

The Israelites were fond of using names that had meaning (as do most people until the names become so common that the original meaning is forgotten). In the Bible, it was also traditional to name a child after some event in connection with his birth. The Hebrew version of the name given by Pharaoh's daughter is *Mosheh,* and the Hebrew word *mashah* means "to draw out." The connection, to Hebrew-speaking people, would seem obvious.

However, it seems unlikely that an Egyptian princess would name her adopted son by means of a Hebrew word, the language of slaves. She would be much more likely to give him an Egyptian name, and "Moses" does seem to be such a name. It means "son" in Egyptian. It appears in the names of some of the best-known pharaohs. Thus, Thutmosis is "son of

Thoth," an Egyptian god, while Ramses, or Rameses, is "son of Ra," another Egyptian god.

Egyptian name or not, however, Moses turned out to be the most revered hero of the Israelite tradition, so revered in fact that there was a certain hesitation in using the name afterward. There are fewer Moseses in later Jewish history than there are Jacobs and Abrahams and Josephs.

The name is not altogether absent, however. Moses ben Maimon, better known as Maimonides (my-mon′ih-deez), was a renowned Jewish philosopher of the twelfth century who was born in Moslem Spain and lived out his life in Moslem Egypt. Again, Moses Mendelssohn was a Jewish philosopher of the eighteenth century who lived in Germany. (His grandson was Felix Mendelssohn, the composer.)

Returning to the original Moses, it was the traditional belief of the Jews (a belief which Christians accepted) that Moses was the author of the first five books of the Bible.* For that reason, these five books are sometimes lumped together as "The Books of Moses." The edition of the Authorized Version which I am using calls Genesis "The First Book of

* Modern Biblical scholars believe that the five books were not written by one person but are a combination of several different lines of tradition. They can pick out the different lines by the names used for God, by the type of material involved, and so on. This "higher criticism" need not concern us in this book, however.

Moses, called Genesis," follows that with "The Second Book of Moses, called Exodus," and so on.

A more formal name for the five books of Moses is "Pentateuch" (pen′tah-tyook), from Greek words meaning "five books."

Moses grew up with an Egyptian education and upbringing, but either he knew himself to be an Israelite, or else he simply sympathized with a people in bondage. In any case, he was angered, one day, at the sight of an Egyptian overseer striking an Israelite. He interfered in the matter and killed the Egyptian.

It turned out that this had been witnessed and Moses felt it would not be safe to remain in Egypt. For that reason, he traveled eastward into the land of Midian, which is usually thought of as being located on the northwestern edge of the Arabian peninsula. There the power of Pharaoh did not extend.

In Midian, Moses met and married Zipporah (zih-poh′ruh, meaning "bird" in Hebrew), the daughter of Reuel (roo′el, meaning "God is his friend"), a Midianite priest. There is some confusion about the name of Moses' father-in-law, for a few verses later he is called Jethro (jeth′roh). Perhaps he was known by both names, as Jacob was also known as Israel, or perhaps one of the names was a title.

Moses had a son named Gershom (gur′shum) and

might have settled down for the rest of his life as a shepherd and herdsman, but events were marching on in Egypt. There the "Pharaoh of the Oppression" (Ramses II?) had died and a new Pharaoh had come to the throne (Merneptah?), often called the Pharaoh of the Exodus because it was under him that the Israelites left Egypt.

If Merneptah is the Pharaoh of the Exodus, then the Exodus must have taken place about 1215 B.C., or almost three hundred years after the traditional date of 1491 B.C. set by Ussher.

The description of the turning point in Moses' life begins with:

> Ex.3:1. *Now Moses kept the flock of Jethro his father in law, the priest of Midian: and he led the flock to the backside of the desert, and came to the mountain of God, even to Horeb.*

The mountain here referred to as "Horeb" (hore′-eb) is considered to be the same as the mountain spoken of in other places in Exodus as "Sinai" (sigh′-nigh). It is called "the mountain of God" because, through much of Biblical history, this mountain was associated with God. In particular, it was at Mount Sinai that the Israelites were to receive the most important revelation of the Old Testament.

Exactly where Mount Sinai (or Horeb) is located has been a matter of dispute. Since Moses was living in Midian at the time, it might seen natural to have the mountain in Midian, too.

However, the verse says that Moses led the flock "to the backside of the desert." The Revised Standard Version has Moses lead the flock "to the west side of the wilderness."

Well, Midian borders on the Gulf of Akaba (uh-kah′buh), which is the northeasternmost inlet of the Red Sea. The Gulf is to the west of Midian, and the other side of the narrow stretch of water might be considered the "back side" or the "west side" of the wilderness. On this west side is a triangular peninsula lying between Egypt and Arabia (see map on page 197).

Near the southern tip of the peninsula is a mountain range. A particular peak of this mountain range, one which is about a mile and a half high, is usually identified as Mount Sinai. In Arabic, its name is *Jebel Musa* (jeb′el moo′suh, "Mount of Moses"). The mountain has given its name to the entire triangular stretch of land on which it stands, which is now known as the Sinai Peninsula. (Nowadays, it is part of Egypt.)

The name of Sinai has turned up in modern times in a very dramatic way. The story is as follows:

Because of the connection with the Bible, Mount Sinai has always been much revered, and as long ago as the sixth century A.D., churches and monasteries were established on its slopes.

In 1844, a German scholar named Konstantin von Tischendorf was exploring antiquities in the Near East at the request of the Russian czar, Alexander II. In the Monastery of St. Catherine on Mount Sinai, he came across an old copy of the Bible, a very old one, containing most of the Old Testament and every word of the New. It is supposed to date back to the fourth century A.D. and to this day is the oldest complete copy of the New Testament ever discovered.

This old Bible was named the Codex Sinaiticus. The term "codex" is applied to large, old books, so the name means "old book from Sinai."

After much persuasion the monks loaned the book to Alexander II in 1869. It was kept in Russia thereafter. After the Russian Revolution, the Soviet government, which badly needed money and was not impressed with old Bibles, sold it to the British museum in 1933, for half a million dollars!

Moses, on the slopes of Mount Sinai, found no old manuscript, but came across something considerably more wonderful:

> Ex.3:2. *And the angel of the Lord appeared unto him in a flame of fire out of the midst of a bush: and he looked, and, behold, the bush burned with fire, and the bush was not consumed.*

The picture of the burning bush is a dramatic one, and people have not been able to resist applying it to certain bushes with very colorful flowers. A bush called the wahoo, for instance, has rich purple-red flowers which give it the appearance of having broken out into flame when it is blooming. For that reason a popular name for the plant is "burning bush."

Of course, the burning bush can be interpreted less literally, too. People who withstand and survive periods of savage persecution (such as the Jews themselves) might well consider themselves to be symbolized by the bush. They have been subjected to the fire of persecution and yet were not consumed. The Church of Scotland, too, at the end of the seventeenth century, felt this. The church members had survived what they considered to have been an era of great danger and persecution, so they took as their emblem the burning bush, with the motto *Nec tamen consumebatur*. The motto is the Latin for "nevertheless it was not consumed."

Moses approached the bush, but the voice of God came to him from its midst and warned him to come no closer. God then announced that he was going to liberate the Israelites from slavery:

> Ex.3:8. *. . . and . . . bring them . . . unto a good land and a large, unto a land flowing with milk and honey; unto the place of the Ca-*

*naanites, and the Hittites, and the Amorites, and the Perizzites, and the Hivites, and the Jebusites.*

To the ancient peoples of the Near East, milk was much prized as a drink since good water was rather scarce. Honey was a delightful article of diet in the days when refined sugar did not exist and when, therefore, there was no candy or pastry in the modern sense. To say a land is flowing with milk and honey was a dramatic way, then, of saying it was fertile and would produce all the good things in life for those who lived there. Because of its use in the Bible, the phrase is still used to describe any very desirable place; sometimes even to represent heaven itself.

Although the land to which the Israelites were later brought would not seem large and fertile and rich to people used to the Iowa farmlands, for instance, it certainly seemed rich to anyone arriving from the desert. What's more, it supported a large and vigorous population in ancient times.

In the Middle Ages, when the land of milk and honey was under the control of the Mohammedan Arabs and, later, the Mohammedan Turks, the exiled Jews and the distant Christians alike thought of it as perhaps far more fertile and wonderful than it was. Under the Turks, particularly, it was allowed to run down to a poverty-stricken, depopulated desert area.

Once the new nation of Israel was established in 1948 over parts of the area, heroic efforts were made to irrigate and renovate the land. Considerable success was achieved too, and the desert began to bloom. Thus, in 1961, when a musical comedy opened on Broadway concerning American women on a visit to Israel, it took as its title *Milk and Honey*.

The land of milk and honey to which God refers in Ex.3:8 is next identified by its inhabitants. "Canaanites" is a general name for the people who live in Canaan (Kay′nen), but sometimes it is used particularly for those who inhabit the lowlands. The other five names are more restricted.

The Hittites represent the remnants of a mighty empire which ruled over much of what is now Turkey. The Hittite Empire was at its height from 1550 to 1250 B.C., or just at the time of the eighteenth and nineteenth dynasties of Egypt. In fact, Ramses II fought a great battle in Syria against the Hittites and got rather the worse of it. If Ramses II were indeed the Pharaoh of the Oppression, it is not surprising that, in the time of Moses, there were groups of Hittites who had penetrated as far south as Canaan. (Hittites are mentioned as being among the inhabitants of Canaan as far back as the time of Abraham. Later on, they are mentioned even in the time of David.)

The Hittite Empire entered its decline during the chaotic times in which the Peoples of the Sea were attacking various areas in the Near East. If Merneptah was indeed the Pharaoh of the Exodus, it was during his reign that this took place, and Canaan would then be comparatively free of the influence of both Egyptians and Hittites. Both of them would be having their hands full elsewhere.

The Amorites were a people who dominated the area of Canaan and beyond before the rise to power of the Hittites and of the Egyptians of the eighteenth dynasty. In 1900 B.C., during the Egyptian Middle Kingdom and the traditional time of Abraham, the Amorites were sufficiently powerful to dominate the great land of Babylonia.

The most famous Babylonian ruler of the time was Hammurabi (hahm′oo-rah′bee), who ruled about 1800 B.C. He rose to particular fame in A.D. 1901 when an inscription in stone containing a detailed code of laws dating back to his time was discovered. It is the oldest known law-code. Well, Hammurabi was an Amorite.

Amorite power broke, however, after 1600 B.C. under the onslaught of growing Hittite power.

The Perizzites (per′ih-zites), Hivites (hy′vites), and Jebusites (jeb′yoo-zites) were minor groups. The Jebusites are important chiefly because they lived in a town called Jebus (jee′bus). This town, after it was taken by the Israelites, centuries later, was renamed Jerusalem.

Having described the land, God went on to say that it was Moses who would lead the children of Israel from Egypt to Canaan. Moses was not enthusiastic. He felt he would not be equal to the task and he was uncertain whether the Israelites would listen to him. The Egyptians believed in numerous gods and every other people of the day had a list of gods just as numerous. In those days, therefore, it was simply impossible to speak of *a* god; one had to know the exact name.

Moses therefore asked the name he was to use and God gave him the necessary information:

> Ex.3:14. *And God said unto Moses, I AM THAT I AM: and he said, Thus shalt thou say unto the children of Israel, I AM hath sent me unto you.*

The phrase "I AM THAT I AM" is a little puzzling as ordinary English, and the Revised Standard Version has it "I AM WHO I AM." In a footnote, it offers two other possibilities, "I AM WHAT I AM" and "I WILL BE WHAT I WILL BE."

The gist seems to be that God cannot be defined

or explained. He is what He is and this is all a man can understand. Furthermore, when He calls Himself "I AM," He emphasizes His existence. He is something that exists. Everything else in the Universe was created and there was, therefore, a time in the past when it didn't exist. There might well be a time in the future when all else will no longer exist. God, however, *exists,* always and forever.

It is possible that this notion of existence, of I AM-ness, is the root of the Hebrew word "Yahveh," which is the name of God in the Bible.* Another way of expressing the notion of existence forever is to say that something is "eternal." This word comes from a Latin word for "an age," that is, for an indefinitely long period of time. And, indeed, one of the ways we sometimes refer to God is as "the Eternal." That may be a good translation into English of "Yahveh."

When God points out that He is "Existence," that implies that other gods, if they exist at all, are created by God just as everything else in the Universe was. The various gods worshiped by the Egyptians and other peoples, therefore, cannot be gods like God.

Because of this and because of other verses in the

---

* The word "Yahveh" was twisted through a series of events into "Jehovah." How this happened is discussed in *Words in Genesis.*

books of Moses, it is sometimes said that it was Moses who taught monotheism to the Israelites. If this took place in the reign of Merneptah, then Moses lived 150 years after the monotheist Pharaoh, Ikhnaton. There are people who suggest that Moses may have learned his monotheism from traditions concerning Ikhnaton. On the other hand, Jews trace monotheism back to Abraham, whose lifetime, traditionally, was many centuries before Ikhnaton.

Moses still doubted his ability to carry conviction to the Israelites, however, and so God decided to give him a proof. He made it possible for him to perform a feat outside the ordinary course of nature.

Now, even primitive men recognized that the universe, if left to itself, followed a fixed pattern. Stones fell downward, not upward, for instance; trees remained rooted in place and did not speak; birds might fly but men could not, and so on. Whenever something occurred that seemed not to follow the fixed pattern of nature, it was beyond or above nature. The Latin prefix "super-" means "above" and so such an event was "supernatural."

Any beings that were not subject to the ordinary course of the laws of nature, or could cause natural objects to act in defiance of those laws were themselves supernatural. Thus, God and angels are supernatural. To those early peoples who believed that ghosts, demons, and spirits, generally, have such powers, those were "supernatural" too.

The particular supernatural power given Moses is described:

> Ex.4:2. *And the Lord said unto him, What is that in thine hand? And he said, A rod.*
>
> Ex.4:3. *And he said, Cast it on the ground. And he cast it on the ground, and it became a serpent; and Moses fled from before it.*
>
> Ex.4:4. *And the Lord said unto Moses, Put forth thine hand, and take it by the tail. And he put forth his hand, and caught it, and it became a rod in his hand:*

Such a supernatural event is something that would naturally cause wonder. In fact, such an event is often described as "a wonder." The Latin word for "to wonder" is *mirare*, and from that is derived the word "miracle," to describe such an event as turning a rod into a serpent and back again.

The miraculous events in the Bible and in later legends were always very impressive to people, just as anything very unusual would be expected to be. During the Middle Ages, folk plays were presented concerning passages from the Bible and from the lives of Christian saints. Such passages and lives were always filled with interesting supernatural events, so that they came to be called "miracle plays."

As for the specific miracle described here, it converted Moses' rod into a special kind of magical object in the minds of many people. This was particularly so since later on in the books of Moses it was to be involved in other miraculous occurrences.

There is, for instance, a kind of superstitious ritual carried on by some people, which involves a forked hazel twig or something of that sort. It is supposed to dip of its own accord when it is passed over underground water, or a vein of gold, or something that is lost.

Now the word "divine" is from a Latin word meaning "pertaining to a god." In English, therefore, it means godlike. The voice from the burning bush might be called the Divine Voice, for instance. (This has been cheapened into meaning something that is merely very pleasant, as when a young lady might describe a party or a movie by saying, "It was just divine.") On the other hand, since one of the godlike powers that was most important to ancient peoples was the ability to foretell the future, the phrase "to divine" meant to do just that. And a twig that could give information that could not be discovered by natural means would be a "divining rod."

However, because of the events in the Book of

Exodus, a divining rod is sometimes referred to as "Moses' rod."

Even yet, Moses was reluctant. Now he pleaded that he was a slow speaker and not eloquent. By this time God was impatient and he made use of one final persuasion:

> Ex.4:14. . . . *and he said, Is not Aaron the Levite thy brother? I know that he can speak well. And also, behold, he cometh forth to meet thee: . . .*

This is the first appearance of Aaron in the Bible. A later verse in the Bible makes it clear that he was three years older than Moses, so he must have been born before Pharaoh's order that all the Israelite boy-babies be drowned. He is described as "the Levite" (lee′vite), meaning a descendant of Levi, third son of Jacob.

To be sure, Moses, as Aaron's brother, was also a Levite, but the word had special meaning in Aaron's case. Later, Aaron was to become the first high priest of Israel, and the position of high priest and of all the subsidiary functions of priesthood was to remain in his family. Because all priests were Levites, the word "Levite" became synonymous with "priest." The phrase "Aaron the Levite," therefore, is but another way of saying "Aaron the priest," even though he had not yet become the high priest.

"Aaron," by the way, is a fairly common name in modern times even among non-Jews. The most famous Aaron in American history is Aaron Burr, who was a senator from New York from 1791 to 1797 and the Vice-President of the United States from 1801 to 1805.

Both Moses and Aaron were revered as prophets by the Mohammedans, as well as by the Jews and Christians. The Mohammedan form of "Moses" is written "Musa" in English. Thus, the Arabic general who conquered Spain in the early eighth century A.D. was Musa ibn-Nusayr (moo′sah ib-n noo-sire′). The Arabic version of "Aaron" is far better known to the west through the collection of stories called *The Thousand and One Nights* (or *The Arabian Nights*). The Caliph who figures in many of these stories, and who, in actual history, was the most powerful of all Mohammedan rulers, was Harun al-Raschid (hah-roon′ ar′rah-sheed′), which in English would be "Aaron the Just."

With Aaron as his spokesman, Moses could find no further excuse. He said farewell to his father-in-law, took his wife and children and, with Aaron, returned to Egypt and delivered his message to the Israelites.

It was next necessary to face Pharaoh.

# 3

## Pharaoh

MOSES AND AARON confront Pharaoh first with the request that the Israelites be allowed a temporary leave:

> Ex.5:1. *And afterward Moses and Aaron went in, and told Pharaoh, Thus saith the Lord God of Israel, Let my people go, that they may hold a feast unto me in the wilderness.*

The word "feast" comes from the Latin *festa*, meaning "holiday." It refers to a joyous celebration in gratitude for the good done mankind by some divine being. Such a celebration is naturally accompanied by good eating, particularly since the first festivals may have been to celebrate a successful harvest. For that reason, "feast" is often used, nowadays, to mean a large meal of many courses, whether religion is involved or not.

The Spanish equivalent, *fiesta*, and the French *fête* are also familiar to English-speaking people as words signifying times of gaiety and merriment. So is the allied English word "festival," so that "festal" and "festive" mean merry and gay. In ancient times (and in modern times, too), feasts meant flowers as well as food, and the revelers wore garlands. For that reason, something that is draped with garlands or ribbons is said to be "festooned."

Now the story of the conflict between Moses and Pharaoh that follows upon this initial request has always been thrilling and dramatic not only to modern Jews, but also to a people who in their turn had known slavery and oppression — the Negroes brought to this country from Africa and forced into slavery. They composed simple and stirring songs interpreting the stories of the Bible to themselves, and one of the most powerful and best known is the spiritual, "Go down, Moses" with its strong, slow refrain, "Let my people go," taken directly from this verse.

Pharaoh would have none of Moses' request, however:

> Ex.5:4. *And the king of Egypt said unto them, Wherefore do ye, Moses and Aaron, let the people from their works? get you unto your burdens.*

Now the Authorized Version of the Bible is full of what are called "archaisms" (from a Greek word meaning "old"). Archaisms are old-fashioned word usages that are no longer part of the common speech. We are quite used to many archaisms (mainly because they occur in the Bible) so that we understand them, even though we don't use them in our own conversation. Archaisms can even be useful, for when Biblical language is not quite like ordinary speech, it takes on a kind of stately dignity.

The most common archaism of the Bible involves its use of the second person pronoun. There was a time when it was common in English to use the pronoun "thou" when addressing one person, and "you" when addressing more than one person. (In the same way, French has *tu* and *vous*, and German has *du* and *ihr*. In fact, the words "thou," *tu* and *du* are all closely related.)

However, people have always found it necessary to show obvious signs of respect to people over them, to use titles or special formulas. Once this is done, it becomes embarrassing and even insulting to use a simple pronoun. In speaking to a king, one would say, "I thank Your Majesty" instead of "I thank thee."

The effort to show respect and to be polite eventually made it impossible to say simply "thou" and "thee" to anyone except close relatives and dear friends. It was only to such people that the French would say *tu* or the Germans *du*. It was also used to children, servants, and inferiors to whom no respect was due, and that, more than ever, made the pronoun seem disrespectful.

Consequently, the Frenchman will use the second person plural and say *vous*, even when he is speaking to only one person, if that person is someone to whom ordinary respect must be shown. It is as though by seeming to spread the pronoun out among a number of people, one is more polite than if one addressed a single individual directly with a pronoun.

For modern Germans, even the second person plural seems too direct. They use the third person plural and say *Sie* (which really means "they") when they want to address someone respectfully by means of a pronoun.

In English, the second person plural, "you," is used, as in French, even though a single person is addressed. The English language went further than either French or German in one respect, however, for it wiped out the second person singular completely. It is no longer used even to the dearest friend or to a child or to a servant. Everyone is "you."

The Authorized Version, however, makes use of the second person singular and of the forms of the verb that go with it. It says "thou hast," "thou goest," and "thou art," instead of "you have," "you go," and "you are." It says "I gave thee" instead of "I gave you." It says "thy servants" instead of "your servants," and "it is thine" instead of "it is yours."

Because of this frequent use in the Bible, the second person singular remains a living part of the language even though we don't use it in ordinary speech. In fact, because of its association with the Bible, it has come to seem fit only for elevated, lofty, and poetic thoughts, so that preachers, when they offer a prayer, immediately switch to "thou" and "thee" as though it would be impolite to say "you" to God — which is just the reverse of the usual feeling.

The Revised Standard Version changes most of the *thou*'s and *thee*'s to "you," but keeps the second person singular when God is being addressed.

There is, I should say, a specialized case, but one related to religion, where the second person singular is still used in ordinary speech. In the mid-seventeenth century, an Englishman named George Fox founded a "Society of Friends" dedicated to the practice of great simplicity in religion. They felt that no man should be shown the respect due a superior, since all men were equal in the sight of God. Therefore, one ought not to remove one's hat before another, and one ought not to use titles, but to address everyone as "Friend."

Since the use of the second person plural, when addressing one person, was itself a sign of respect, the Society of Friends insisted on the second person singular to everyone, even to the king. The custom grew among them, however, to use the objective case of the pronoun only, and to say "thee art" instead of "thou art." This is grammatically wrong, but they did it anyway.

George Fox at one time warned a judge, before whom he was brought, to "tremble at the word of the Lord." For that reason he and his followers were sarcastically called Quakers (that is, people who quaked, or trembled). They accepted the name and it is as "Quakers" that they are generally known today, although the official name of their sect is still the Society of Friends.

In the verse I have quoted, 5:4, "thou" and "thee" are not used because Pharaoh is addressing both Moses and Aaron and the second person plural is used. However it contains a "ye," which is another form of "you," an archaic form originally meant as a plural but often used as a singular. It is found in the Bible but is not used in common speech. The Revised Standard Version changes all *ye*'s to *you*'s.

The word "unto" is also archaic, and in modern English (and in the Revised Standard Version) is expressed simply as "to."

The reason I have brought up archaisms in connection with this verse, however, is that it contains two examples which are not only not used today, but which are so unfamiliar as actually to raise the chance of misunderstanding.

For instance, Pharaoh asks Moses and Aaron why they "let the people from their works."

In this case, the word "let" means "to hinder" or "to prevent." This is not only a meaning that is no longer in current use, but it is precisely the reverse of the usual meaning of "let" which is "to permit" or "to allow." Thus, to say "Let my people go" means "allow them to go," while "Let my people from going" would mean "do not allow them to go."

The archaic meaning of "let" still exists in the legal phrase "without let or hindrance" meaning that there is to be no barrier of any kind to whatever is being discussed. (The legal profession, which must stick closely to tradition, makes use of as many archaisms as the Authorized Version — at least.) Again, in tennis, the failure to return a ball because of some hindrance that prevents a fair chance at a return is called a "let."

The Revised Standard Version eliminates confusion by using "let" only in the modern sense. It says "Let my people go" in Ex.5:1, but "Why do you take the people away from their work?" in 5:4.

Notice that in the last phrase, the Revised Standard Version changes the "wherefore" of the Authorized Version into "why." The word "wherefore" means "why" but it has become old-fashioned and is rarely used. In fact, people who rarely hear "wherefore" put to proper use sometimes concentrate on the first syllable and think that it means "where."

Thus, in the famous balcony scene in *Romeo and Juliet*, Juliet comes out on the balcony and wonders, wistfully, why Romeo, with whom she has fallen desperately in love, has to be a member of a family with whom her own family is having a feud to the death. She begins a tender soliloquy with "O Romeo, Romeo! wherefore art thou Romeo?" meaning "Why must you be Romeo? Why couldn't you have belonged to some other family?"

Yet to most people not very familiar with the play, the line seems to be "Where art thou, Romeo?" Therefore, on TV, whenever the scene is presented humorously (and it often is), Juliet is always made to behave as though she were bellowing, "Where are you, Romeo? Yoo hoo, Romeo."

This spoils the whole beautiful scene and it is to avoid such mistakes in understanding the Bible (which is, of course, more important, even, than Shakespeare) that the Revised Standard Version has eliminated as many archaisms as possible.

The first exchange between Moses and Pharaoh ends in further trouble for the Israelites:

> Ex.5:6. *And Pharaoh commanded the same day the taskmasters of the people, and their officers, saying,*
>
> Ex.5:7. *Ye shall no more give the people straw to make brick, as heretofore: let them go and gather straw for themselves.*
>
> Ex.5:8. *And the tale of the bricks, which they did make heretofore, ye shall lay upon them; ye shall not diminish aught thereof: . . .*

The straw in brickmaking is used as a binder in the clay to make stronger brick. Without the straw, it would be difficult or impossible to make satisfactory bricks. Despite the time lost in gathering straw, the day's "tale" of bricks was kept the same. The word "tale" is an old-fashioned one for "number." We still keep a form of the word in "tally." The Revised Standard Version changes the phrase to "the number of bricks."

As a consequence of these verses, "to make bricks without straw" has become a common phrase used to describe any effort to do something without the actual means or capacity to do it.

The Israelites could not turn out the usual quantity of bricks while having to collect their own straw, so they were beaten. Naturally, they blamed Moses and Aaron for this, feeling that their interference had but made matters worse. Moses and Aaron in turn complained to God.

God, however, repeated his promise to liberate the Israelites and bring them to Canaan:

> Ex.6:6. . . . *and I will redeem you with a stretched out arm* . . .

"Redeem" is from a Latin word meaning "to take back." Thus, you redeem a watch that has been pawned. The Israelites had been given to the Egyptians for a while and now God was going to take them back. Hence he is occasionally referred to in later books of the Old Testament as "the Redeemer."

Once God had renewed this promise of rescue, he ordered Moses and Aaron to approach Pharaoh again.

At this point the story is interrupted in order that the genealogy of the family of Levi be given. In the listing, Levi's second son is Kohath, whose oldest son is Amram, and he, in turn, is the father of Moses and Aaron. Thus, Moses and Aaron are the great-grandsons of Levi and the great-great-grandsons of Jacob.

The children and grandchildren of Aaron are then given because they are important in the later history of the priesthood:

> Ex.6:23. *And Aaron took him Elisheba . . . to wife; and she bare him Nadab, and Abihu, Eleazar, and Ithamar. . . .*
>
> Ex.6:25. *And Eleazar . . . took him one of the daughters of Putiel to wife; and she bare him Phinehas: . . .*

Aaron's wife, Elisheba (ee-lish′ee-bah, meaning "God is an oath"), has a name that may seem unfamiliar to us, but it appears in the New Testament in a Greek form. This is Elisabeth (or Elizabeth). The name of the mother of John the Baptist, it became popular throughout Christian lands. An empress of Austria was named Elizabeth, and queens of Hungary and Belgium bore the name.

The most famous Elizabeth, however, was Elizabeth I of England who ruled from 1558 to 1603. This was the golden age of English literature (the time of Shakespeare and of others nearly as great), a time of internal peace after years of unrest, and a time of victory over the Spanish Armada. The expression "Elizabethan Age" has therefore come almost to mean a Golden Age. The present monarch of England is Elizabeth II.

The popularity of the name Elizabeth is also shown by the number of diminutives obtained from it. There is "Eliza," "Elissa," "Elsie," "Liz," "Lizzie," "Lisa," "Libby," "Beth," "Bess," "Bessie," "Betsy," and "Betty."

Eleazar (el′ee-ay′zar) and Phinehas (fin′ee-as), the son and grandson of Aaron who eventually succeeded to the high priesthood, are examples of names that were moderately popular among later Jews. Several other individuals in the Old Testament are named Eleazar (which means "God has helped"), but there is no mention of one in the New Testament, except in the list of ancestors of Joseph, the husband of the Virgin Mary. His great-grandfather is an Eleazar.

Phinehas (which is probably an Egyptian name to begin with) does not occur in the New Testament at all. The name is better known to us in the version "Phineas." The Hebrew version of Phinehas is

"Pinkhas" (where the *kh* represents the German guttural *ch*). The name "Pincus," which is sometimes found as either the first name or the last name of modern Jews, is a version of this.

When Moses and Aaron faced Pharaoh a second time, it was with more than a simple request. They brought evidence of supernatural power:

> Ex.7:10. . . . *Aaron cast down his rod before Pharaoh . . . and it became a serpent.*
> Ex.7:11. *Then Pharaoh also called the wise men and the sorcerers: now the magicians of Egypt, they also did in like manner with their enchantments.*
> Ex.7:12. *For they cast down every man his rod, and they became serpents: but Aaron's rod swallowed up their rods.*

Because of this passage, "Aaron's rod" can be used as the equivalent of "Moses' rod." In addition, the expression "Aaron's serpent" refers to something so powerful as to eliminate lesser objects of the same sort.

The Egyptians who competed with Moses and Aaron are labeled "wise men." In ancient times, it seemed important to know how to understand and control the supernatural, as today it seems important to know how to understand and control science. The supernatural in ancient times, and science now, are methods of getting things done that cannot be done with the bare hands. The ancients believed themselves as dependent on the supernatural for the growing of crops and the warding off of disease as we believe ourselves to be dependent on fertilizer and antibiotics.

Consequently, to us it is the scientist who is a "wise man," while to the ancients it was the man who knew how to control supernatural forces. The importance of these men was such that there are many terms in the language that could be applied to them. "Sorcerer" comes from a Latin word meaning "lot" (in the sense of a man's lot in life). A sorcerer, in other words, is one who could foretell a man's fate by his knowledge of the supernatural.

"Magician" is from a Persian word for a priest. One of the functions of priests everywhere is to pray for good things and to perform various rituals designed to please the various gods. Their knowledge of such rituals gave them the power, presumably, to bring about desirable events in a supernatural manner.

The recital of the necessary form of words that could force human will on supernatural beings was usually in the form of a singsong. (It is easier to memorize a pattern of words exactly if you sing it.

Most of us remember the exact words to dozens of songs, but can recite hardly any prose.) The Latin word for "to sing" is *cantare*, therefore the spells cast by magicians are "incantations" or "enchantments" and a magician is an "enchanter" (one who "chants" his spells). The word "charm" comes from a Latin word meaning "a song," so an enchanter can cast a charm upon you. This may be for your benefit, as when you are protected from harm and therefore have a "charmed life."

The fact that Egyptian magicians in particular would be skillful in their arts would not be surprising to the ancients. The old traditions of Egypt and the mighty structures it had built were evidence enough that Egyptians had learned more than the younger civilizations about such things. Besides, Egyptians knew a great deal about the movements of the heavenly bodies and had developed intricate systems of astrology; that is, the foretelling of the future by means of the changing positions of the planets.

There is still a faint remnant of this ancient reputation of Egypt in the language. The phrase "Egyptian days" is sometimes used to mean "unlucky days." This is because the Egyptian astrologers listed two days in each month that were especially unlucky and on which no chances were to be taken. Before we laugh at this, we might think of our own feelings toward some innocent Friday that happens to fall on the thirteenth day of the month.

Since his own magicians had duplicated the feats of Moses and Aaron, Pharaoh was not worried. It was therefore necessary to tighten the screw a bit further. God's instructions began:

> Ex.7:15. *Get thee unto Pharaoh in the morning; lo, he goeth out unto the water . . .*

The word "lo" is an archaism that is apparently a contraction of the Anglo-Saxon word *loken*, meaning "look" or "see." Another old-fashioned word with the same meaning is "behold." Thus, in Ex.4:14, where God tells Moses that Aaron is on his way to meet him, He says, ". . . behold, he cometh forth to meet thee . . ."

Although we practically never use either word in ordinary speech, the influence of the Bible is such that sometimes when we want to be very impressive we will say, "Lo and behold!" when what we mean in plain modern English is "Look at that!"

Notice that the verse also contains the expression "he goeth." This is a good time, then, to mention that some centuries ago it was common to end the third person singular of a verb in *-th* rather than in *-s*. Thus, one would once have said "he hath," "he doth," and "he goeth," where we now say "he has," "he does," and "he goes." The Revised Standard Version uses the modern form of the third person singular.

With God's new instructions, a series of dramatic calamities struck the Egyptians, one after the other. After each of them, Pharaoh in fright agreed to allow the Israelites to leave and the calamity was removed. But then, with normalcy restored, Pharaoh would change his mind and refuse to let the Israelites go.

There were ten of these calamities altogether and they are commonly referred to as the "ten plagues of Egypt." The word "plague" comes from a Latin expression meaning "blow" or "stroke" and can refer to any unexpected misfortune that strikes without warning. Thus, we will commonly say "a stroke of bad luck."

The old-fashioned expressions "plague take it" and "a plague on him" voice the unkind wish that misfortune might befall something or someone.

In past centuries, one of the most common varieties of a misfortune striking without warning was an infectious disease. Before the days of modern medicine, an infectious disease might spread from one to another like an irresistible flood, killing large numbers.

Scarcely anything can be so terrifying and make one feel so helpless. Plague came to be applied most often to epidemic diseases that spread quickly and struck hard. The most terrifying of all epidemics ever to hit Europe was the "Black Death" which swept the continent in the mid-fourteenth century. It, more than any other disease, is the "Plague." There are two varieties, the "bubonic plague," which is spread by lice and by the rats that carry the lice; and "pneumonic plague," that spreads directly from man to man.

Another word for plague is "pest," or "pestilence." This comes from the Latin, but its original meaning is uncertain. However, the germ that causes plague is "Pasteurella pestis." ("Pasteurella" is named in honor of Louis Pasteur, who first put forth the germ theory of disease. It is a dubious memorial but it is meant as an honor.)

However, partly because of the famous story of the plagues of Egypt, the word "plague" has never been entirely confined to one disease or even to epidemic diseases in general. Since a number of the Egyptian plagues dealt with an overabundance of different kinds of annoying creatures, we still speak of a "plague of locusts" or a "plague of flies" when we mean that the creatures are swarming in unbearable quantity.

Many kinds of living creatures that can swarm in large numbers and thereby become harmful are referred to as "pests." The rabbit makes a nice pet in the United States but is an unbearable pest in Australia. The extra *s* makes a difference.

The word "pest" has been weakened by being applied to minor nuisances. It is probably used more to refer to a little brother or sister than to any other object. We speak of something that is only a bother as "pestilential," "pestiferous" or even, in a kind of baby talk, as "pesky." And to bother is to "pester."

The first nine plagues of Egypt may be summarized as follows:

1) The water of the Nile River was turned to blood and remained so for seven days. The Egyptians had to dig wells to get drinkable water. The magicians duplicated this and Pharaoh remained adamant.

2) Frogs were multiplied in the land. The magicians duplicated this, too, but that did Pharaoh no good. He therefore asked Moses and Aaron to remove the plague, offering to let the Israelites go into the wilderness and sacrifice to God. Moses and Aaron did so, and then Pharaoh changed his mind.

3) Lice were multiplied in the land. This the magicians could not duplicate and they agreed that a supernatural power stronger than those at their command was involved:

> Ex.8:19. *Then the magicians said unto Pharaoh, This is the finger of God: . . .*

This is a dramatic picture of God's power since he can perform wonders by the mere exertion of a finger. The phrase "finger of God" may therefore be used to describe any event that seems to be out of the ordinary, especially if it seems to have a kind of divine justice to it. Sometimes, where people hesitate to involve God, they will say "finger of Fate" instead.

However, the despair of the magicians did not affect Pharaoh. He would not budge.

4) Flies were multiplied in the land. Now Pharaoh suggested that the Israelites sacrifice to God in Egypt, without going out into the wilderness. Moses, however, objected to this:

> Ex.8:26. *And Moses said, It is not meet so to do; for we shall sacrifice the abomination of the Egyptians . . .*

The word "meet" is an archaic one meaning "fitting" and the Revised Standard Version puts the phrase into the more modern-sounding "It would not be right to do so."

The word "abomination" is derived from Latin words meaning "away from the omen." In other words, it is something from which you should turn away because it is a bad omen. In an age when people really believed in omens, a bad one could be a very seriously depressing thing. Imagine being certain that you would suffer extreme misfortune because an omen said so. That would be an "ominous" situation.

You can well understand that a person would hate a bad omen with all his heart and turn from it with a feeling of disgust, loathing, and despair. For that reason "abomination" came to mean anything that was completely repellent.

To people who take the rituals of their religion seriously, there is nothing so repellent and loathsome — so abominable, in other words — as something that violates those rituals. To the Egyptian, for instance, certain animals were sacred and could not be harmed. The Israelites, however, would sacrifice such animals and this deed would be an abomination to the Egyptians. Moses pointed out that it would not be right to offend the Egyptians so; and, in fact, it would not have been safe to do so.

Pharaoh therefore agreed to let the Israelites sacrifice at three days' journey from Egypt's settled regions, and the flies were removed. Again, Pharaoh changed his mind.

5) This was the first that involved disease, and God instructed Moses to warn of the plague thus:

> Ex.9:3. *Behold, the hand of the Lord is upon thy cattle . . . there shall be a very grievous murrain.*

The word "murrain" (mur′in) is used only here in the Bible. It comes from a Latin word meaning "to die" and signifies a deadly disease. It is equivalent to "plague," and the Hebrew word which is translated here as "murrain" is translated elsewhere in the Bible as "pestilence." The Revised Standard Version uses the words "severe plague" instead of "grievous murrain."

About the only other place one is likely to meet the word is in an old-fashioned exclamation such as "A murrain on it," which is identical with "A plague on it."

As a result of the murrain, the cattle of the Egyptians died, but Pharaoh would still not give in.

6) Next, disease touched human beings and there was an outbreak of boils:

> Ex.9:10. *And they took ashes . . . and Moses sprinkled it up toward heaven; and it became a boil breaking forth with blains upon man, and upon beast.*

"Blain" is an archaic word meaning a running sore, and the Revised Standard Version translates the phrase, "it became boils breaking out in sores." (The only time we ever use the word is to describe the rough, red and cracked condition of the skin on hands and feet exposed to continuous cold and damp. These are blains brought on by chill weather — that is "chilblains.") Pharaoh did not let even the boils and blains influence him.

7) Hail was brought down upon the land, together with thunder and lightning. This destroyed all men and beasts that had not taken refuge indoors as a result of a warning by Moses the day before. This time Pharaoh sent for Moses and Aaron and offered to let the Israelites go. The hail was stopped and once again Pharaoh changed his mind.

8) Moses threatened a plague of locusts and Pharaoh's officials now urged that the Israelites be allowed to depart. Pharaoh offered to let the adult males go for the purpose, but Moses insisted that all Israelites must go. The locusts came; Pharaoh gave in; the locusts went; Pharaoh changed his mind.

9) A three-day darkness covered the land, described as follows:

> Ex.10:21. *And the Lord said unto Moses, Stretch out thine hand toward heaven, that there may be darkness over the land of Egypt, even darkness which may be felt.*

This exaggeration of darkness, a "darkness which may be felt," as though it were actually something substantial, was so impressive that the phrase "Egyptian darkness" has come to mean something very dark indeed. On the other hand, the phrase may be literally true. If the darkness were produced by a sandstorm, the sand particles could certainly be felt.

Some people have wondered if this period of darkness might not refer to a total eclipse of the sun that was visible over Egypt on March 27, 1335 B.C. If so, the Exodus could be dated exactly. However, this eclipse was a hundred years before the time of Merneptah, and in any case an eclipse only lasts a few minutes.

At this, Pharaoh offered to let the Israelites sacrifice to God in a body, the women and young included, but insisted that the Israelite cattle remain behind. Moses refused this compromise, too, and the stage was set for the tenth and final plague.

# 4

## Passover

THE FINAL PLAGUE was the one toward which everything had been pointing as a climax. The first nine plagues were merely parlor tricks in comparison. In those ancient times, people believed in a vast number of gods and no one was offended or surprised that another person or tribe might have gods of their own.

The Egyptians were, apparently, quite willing to believe that the Israelites had a God to worship, and were even willing to believe that He was just as real as their own gods. However, since the Israelites were slaves and the Egyptians were masters, it would have seemed logical that the Israelite God must be weaker than the Egyptian gods.

This was common reasoning among many ancient peoples. When one tribe conquered another, the tribal god of the conquerors became the chief god of the area, until the conquerors were defeated in their turn.

In fact, many Israelites seemed to have believed this, too, both at the time of the Exodus and for centuries afterward.* The first nine plagues might be considered as a series of proofs that the Israelite God was more powerful than the Egyptian gods, especially after the first two plagues when the Egyptian magicians could no longer duplicate the feats of Moses and Aaron. This proof was intended as much for the Israelites themselves as for the Egyptians.

With that done, the time for serious business had

---

* The difference was that there were always some Israelites who believed that Yahveh was all-powerful even when the Israelites were defeated and enslaved. Eventually, Israelite prophets made it clear that Yahveh was the *only* God and was the God even of non-Israelites.

come. Moses gave the warning:

> Ex.11:4. *And Moses said, Thus saith the Lord, About midnight will I go out into the midst of Egypt:*
> Ex.11:5. *And all the firstborn in the land of Egypt shall die . . .*

The Negro spiritual "Go Down, Moses," captures the significance of this by adapting the words of the Bible with simple power. There is no mention of any of the plagues but the essential tenth, and the second verse goes:

> . . . "Thus saith the Lord," bold Moses, said,
> "Let my people go!
> If not, I'll strike your firstborn dead,
> Let my people go!"

In the Jewish tradition, it was upon the night of the last plague that they became a nation. Before that, they had been a single family (in the time of Abraham, Isaac, and Jacob) or, in Egypt, nothing more than a horde of slaves.

After the night of the last plague, however, they were free, and left Egypt for a land of their own. Upon that night, then, God begins to instruct Moses as to the manner in which the Israelite nation is to guide its behavior toward God and man.

These instructions are described through the rest of the Book of Exodus and through the remaining three books of the Pentateuch as well. Since the Book of Genesis also contains rules of behavior given by God to men who lived before Moses — to Adam and to Noah, for instance — the entire Pentateuch may be lumped together as "the Law." Because Moses was considered the author of all five books, they are referred to sometimes as "The Law of Moses" or the "Mosaic Law."

The Hebrew word for the Mosaic Law is *Torah*, which means "law." Through the centuries, Jewish scholars have studied the Mosaic Law and amplified it, making deductions from the statements and applying them to changed conditions of life. Eventually, these commentaries were collected into the *Talmud* (a Hebrew word meaning "instruction"). A "Talmudic scholar" would therefore be the Jewish equivalent of a constitutional lawyer.

The first set of instructions, naturally, concerned that very night, the night of the tenth plague, and every anniversary of that night thereafter. It begins:

> Ex.12:2. *This month shall be unto you the beginning of months: it shall be the first month of the year to you.*

Now it is not certain exactly what kind of a calendar the Israelites used at the time of the Exodus, but centuries later, during a period in which they were held captive in Babylon, they adopted the Babylonian calendar (a calendar which the ancient Greeks also borrowed).

This was a lunar calendar in which each month began with the day of the new moon. The time between new moons was either 29 or 30 days, and twelve such lunar months came to 354 days, which is 11¼ days less than the solar year (which modern nations use).

Now the seasons are based on the solar year so that spring begins every 365¼ days. The lunar year loses a little over a month on the seasons every three years. To keep the calendar even with the seasons, the Babylonians (and consequently the Jews and the Greeks) added a thirteenth month every once in a while, according to a fixed pattern.

The month in which the tenth plague took place was originally called Abib. The Jews, however, having adopted the Babylonian calendar, also adopted the Babylonian names for the months. Here is the full list of months:

1) Nisan (March–April)
2) Iyar (April–May)
3) Sivan (May–June)

4) Tammuz (June–July)
5) Ab (July–August)
6) Elul (August–September)
7) Tishri (September–October)
8) Heshvan (October–November)
9) Kislev (November–December)
10) Tebet (December–January)
11) Shebat (January–February)
12) Adar (February–March)

When a thirteenth month becomes necessary, it is put after Adar and is Ve-adar ("second Adar"). The exact day in our own calendar on which the different Hebrew months start can't be given since, the Hebrew calendar being a lunar calendar, the starting days shift from year to year, compared with our solar calendar. The use of the thirteenth month, however, keeps them from shifting too far.

Nisan, which becomes the first month of the year, according to Ex.12:2, begins at the beginning of spring. This is a natural time for people in the North Temperate Zone to begin the year — a time when the fields turn green again and the trees put forth leaves once more; when life seems to be renewed after the temporary death of winter.

This beginning at the vernal equinox was to be found among other peoples, too. The Romans began the year with March 1 until 153 B.C., and the English actually had the year beginning with March 25 until 1752.

Another natural time at which to begin the year is at the autumnal equinox in mid-September. It is harvest time and the food supply is safely gathered or about to be gathered and in a sense the working year is done. You can now begin a new one.

Actually, the Jews have had two New Years, one in Nisan, at the time of the vernal equinox, which is the ecclesiastical New Year, and one in Tishri, at the time of the autumnal equinox, which is the civil New Year. Nowadays the New Year in Tishri is by far the better known, as I shall explain later in the book.

(For that matter, the United States also has two New Years that are, like Nisan and Tishri, six months apart. There is January 1 which is the civil New Year, and July 1 which is the fiscal New Year.)

God's instructions to Moses then deal with the nature of the commemorative feast. The main course is specified:

> Ex.12:3. *Speak ye unto all the congregation of Israel, saying, In the tenth day of this month they shall take to them every man a lamb . . .*

The word "congregation" is from a Latin expression meaning "gather together." The verse pictures all of the Israelites gathered together to listen to Moses' instructions. For that reason, the word is often used in the Bible to mean "all the Israelites." Nowadays, it is most often used to refer to the people who gather together to attend services at one particular church.

During the time of the English Revolution, in the 1640's, there were certain Protestants who felt that each congregation should be independent and decide for itself whom to choose as minister and what rules to follow. These groups called themselves "Congregationalists." The Pilgrims who arrived on the Mayflower and settled in Plymouth in 1620 were Congregationalists.

In the New Testament, the word "synagogue" is used instead of "congregation." "Synagogue" has the same meaning as "congregation" but is derived from the Greek, the original language of the New Testament. Nowadays, however, whereas "congregation" applies to the people within a place of worship (whether Jewish or Christian), "synagogue" is applied to the building itself and is applied only to a Jewish house of worship.

The instructions go on to describe when the lamb is to be killed, how its blood is to be placed on the doorposts, and the manner in which it is to be eaten:

Ex.12:8. *And they shall eat the flesh in that night, roast with fire, and unleavened bread . . .*

By "unleavened bread" is meant bread made without yeast. "Yeast" and "leaven" are synonymous. Both represent that substance (now known to consist of microscopic plant cells) which, when added to bread dough, produces bubbles of gas that raise the dough and make it soft and spongy.

"Yeast" is an old Anglo-Saxon word which may originally arise from an even older Sanskrit word meaning "to boil," since the bubbles that form in the leavened bread resemble bubbles that form when a liquid boils. "Leaven" comes from a Latin word meaning "to raise," since the leavened dough rises up.

Unleavened bread bakes flat and rather cracker-like and, under its Hebrew name of *matzah* (meaning "unleavened"), or *matzoth* in the plural, is to be found in American supermarkets all year round.

A further description of the manner of eating follows:

Ex.12:11. *And thus shall ye eat it; with your loins girded, your shoes on your feet, and your staff in your hand; and ye shall eat it in haste . . .*

The significance is that the next day, after the conclusion of the final plague, the Israelites must be ready to leave Egypt at once and without the least delay. The picture is quite clear except for the phrase "with your loins girded."

In ancient times, most people, including the Israelites, wore gown-like garments, often descending to the ankles. This is fine when one is moving in a stately walk, but if one were to try to walk quickly, the swishing about of the loose garment would interfere. To correct this, it was customary to tie a belt or girdle about the loin (that is, the waist) to make the gown fit more tightly and to make fast walking or work of any kind more practical.

Nowadays, we wear more closely fitting clothes and men almost always wear a belt so that their loins are girded at all times. Nevertheless, because the phrase is used in the Bible, we still sometimes say we will "gird up the loins" when we wish to imply that we are getting ready for hard work.

In the last phrase of the verse, the feast is named:

> Ex.12:11. . . . *it is the Lord's passover.*
>
> Ex.12:12. *For I will pass through the land of Egypt this night, and will smite all the firstborn . . .*
>
> Ex.12:13. . . . *and . . . I will pass over you, and the plague shall not be upon you . . .*

The Hebrew word of which "pass over" is a translation is *pesakh* and this becomes *pascha* in Greek.

In New Testament times, the crucifixion took place during Passover, and Easter, which celebrates the Resurrection three days later, therefore occurs at the same time of the year as does Passover. The exact time of Easter is calculated according to a system that is different from that according to which Passover is calculated, so that they invariably come at slightly different times, a week or so apart. Both are based on the lunar calendar, so that they come at different times from year to year when judged by our own solar calendar.

The word "Easter" has nothing to do with the Resurrection, but is a pagan survival. In the days before Christianity, Anglo-Saxon England celebrated a spring festival in honor of the spring-goddess, Eoster. With the coming of Christianity, the celebration of the Resurrection was substituted, but the old name was kept.

However, the adjective pertaining to Easter is drawn from the Greek version of the original Hebrew word and is "paschal." For instance, the lamb eaten on Passover is the "paschal lamb" and the full moon from which the date of Easter is calculated is called the "paschal full moon."

"Easter," being a Teutonic word, is not found in

the Latin languages, which stick to the proper form. Of particular interest to Americans is the Spanish name of the holiday, *Pascua florida* ("flowery passover" because, it being spring, flowers play an important part in the celebration).

In 1513, the Spanish explorer Ponce de Léon discovered a section of the North American continent on Easter Sunday and he named it for the day — in Spanish, of course — and called it "Florida." Thus, the name of one of our fifty states comes, in very roundabout fashion, from chapter 12, verse 11 of the Book of Exodus.

The instructions continue for an elaborate celebration on each anniversary of the event in future years:

> Ex.12:18. *In the first month, on the fourteenth day of the month at even, ye shall eat unleavened bread, until the one and twentieth day of the month at even.*

"Even" is an old form of "evening," just as "morn" is an old form of "morning." By the Hebrew system, the day begins and ends with sunset. The Jewish Sabbath begins, for instance, on what we would call Friday evening.

A holiday would therefore begin at "even" — at evening, that is — of what we would consider the day *before* the holiday. The first evening of Passover would be, in Hebrew *Erev Pesakh* ("the evening of Passover").

Although our day begins at midnight, and evening is toward the close of a day rather than its beginning, we still sometimes make special note of the evenings before a holiday. It is a hangover from early Christian tradition which, at the very beginning, followed the long Jewish habit. Thus, November 1 is "All Hallows' Day," a day reserved for the commemoration of the saints generally in various Christian sects. The evening of October 31 is therefore "All Hallows' Even," which is abbreviated to "Halloween."

Again, we are all familiar with the evening of December 24 as "Christmas Eve" and with the evening of December 31 as "New Year's Eve."

Returning to Ex.12:18, notice the phrase "one and twentieth." This is an old-fashioned way of saying numbers over twenty. One can say three and thirty (33), six and fifty (56), eight and seventy (78), and so on, placing the units before the tens. It is still done in exactly this fashion in German. In English, however, we have switched the words to place the tens first. The Revised Standard Version switches too, making the phrase read "until the twenty-first day of the month at evening."

In passing the instructions on to the elders of Israel,

Moses goes into further detail concerning the manner of applying the blood to the doorposts.

> Ex.12:22. *And ye shall take a bunch of hyssop, and dip it in the blood . . . and strike the lintel and the two side posts . . .*

The "hyssop" is the English spelling of a Hebrew word that might be more correctly written as "ezob." It is a plant of some sort, and a small one because it is elsewhere in the Bible referred to as growing out of a wall. Because of its use here for sprinkling a fluid (and elsewhere for the purpose of ritual purification), the device used in some churches for sprinkling holy water is sometimes, unofficially, called a hyssop.

The exact type of plant represented by the hyssop is unknown. After the Jews were driven out of their homeland by the Romans, it became first difficult and then impossible for them to remember exactly which plants and animals were meant by this or that Hebrew word. Very often the plants or animals were native to Palestine and were not to be found in their new homes.

There are several small shrubs that are given the name "hyssop" but none of them are likely to be the Biblical hyssop because none are native to Palestine. One likely theory is that the Biblical hyssop is a plant, something like wild thyme, which is abundant in

Palestine and which is called *sa'atar* by the Arabs.

This is a rather minor point, it would seem, but it shows the importance which is atttached to the Bible. Every word in it seems to cry out for a meaning and every point, however minor, is tirelessly explored by scholars.

The protecting effect of the blood is dramatically described.

> Ex.12:23. . . . *the Lord will pass over the door, and will not suffer the destroyer to come in unto your houses to smite you.*

The "destroyer" is death itself. In later times, the Jews pictured an "Angel of Death" with the name Azrael as in particular charge of the end of life, and it is to him that the "destroyer" here is usually taken to apply.

That night, then, the tenth plague was accomplished and death was everywhere in Egypt. Pharaoh's spirit finally broke, and before the night was over, he had sent frantically for Moses and Aaron and ordered them to leave, with the Israelites, both men and women, young and old, and with their flocks and herds:

> Ex.12:37. *And the children of Israel journeyed from Rameses to Succoth, about six hundred thousand on foot that were men, beside children.*

Rameses is, of course, the treasure city they built on the borders of Goshen, as described in chapter 1, verse 11 of the Book of Exodus. Succoth is thought to be a relatively short distance to the east of Rameses and still within the boundaries of Egypt.

Six hundred thousand men would seem to imply a group of people at least two million in number, if the women and children are counted, plus what the Bible describes, in the next verse, as a "mixed multitude" (people of mixed Egyptian and Israelite parentage, perhaps) and a great many cattle.

This seems to be an impossibly large number, and critics try to explain it in various ways, but six hundred thousand adult males is the figure stated.

Further instructions concerning the ritual of the Passover are given and then the matter of the route to Canaan is considered. Looking at the map it would seem that the simplest and shortest route from Egypt to Canaan would be along the coast of the Mediterranean. That undoubtedly was the route followed by Abraham, and by Jacob and his family when they traveled from Canaan to Egypt.

However, something new had been added since Jacob's time, for now, as a result of the invasions of the Peoples of the Sea, the Philistines had swarmed onto the coastal plains of Palestine. (In fact, as I mentioned in *Words in Genesis,* the very word "Palestine" is from "Philistine.")

It was a time when the Iron Age was displacing the Bronze Age. Armies equipped with iron-tipped spears and iron-plated shields could cut their way through other armies equipped only with bronze. The Philistines were iron-armored and the Canaanites could not stand against them and neither, for some centuries, could the Israelites. Therefore:

> Ex.13:17. ... *God led them not through the way of the Philistines, although that was near . . .*
>
> Ex.13:18. *But God led the people about, through the way of the wilderness of the Red sea.*

The Hebrew name for the Red Sea is *Yam suph*, or "Sea of Reeds." The body of water labeled Red Sea on our maps is long and rather narrow (about 1400 miles long but only 130 to 250 miles wide) and lies between Egypt and Arabia. The modern Arabic name for it is *Bahr-el-Hejaz* ("Sea of Hejaz"), after the district of Arabia that borders upon it.

Why is the Red Sea so named? There are theories about that, but no sure reason. Some speculate that it is due to microscopic forms of life that may have once swarmed at certain times and turned the water red. Others think it may be because of reddish shells found on its shores, or the reddish color of the rocks on the Arabian side, or the reddish reflection from the sky, but none of this is convincing.

The name was *Mare Erythraeum* in Greek and Roman days, which is "Red Sea" in Latinized Greek. That name still leaves a trace on the map. In 1882, Italy conquered a section along the southern stretch of the African coast of the Red Sea. It was named "Eritrea," an Italianized version of the Latinized Greek.

The Israelites in heading eastward from Goshen did not approach the main body of the Red Sea. At its northern end, the Red Sea splits into two narrow horn-like projections that lie on either side of the triangular Sinai Peninsula. (See map on page 197.)

The eastern horn is the Gulf of Akaba, about 100 miles long and not much more than ten miles wide at its widest. On the west is what is now known as the Gulf of Suez, which is nearly twice as long and twice as wide as the Gulf of Akaba. It was the Gulf of Suez that the Israelites approached and perhaps not the main body of that either.

Between the northern tip of the Gulf of Suez and the Mediterranean Sea lies an isthmus of land about a hundred miles wide. (It is now called the Isthmus of Suez, and the Suez Canal runs across it.) Near the middle of this isthmus there are, nowadays, tracts of marshy land called the Bitter Lakes. At the time of the Exodus, three thousand years ago and more, the Gulf of Suez seems to have stretched northward to include those Bitter Lakes, forming a shallow pan of water probably filled with reeds. It could well be to this northernmost bit of the Red Sea, not very deep and not more than a couple of miles wide at most, that the name "Sea of Reeds" is applied.

Having reached the Sea of Reeds, the northernmost tip of the Red Sea, the Israelites encamped.

By that time, Pharaoh had recovered his spirit and his iron determination (and surely no man has ever been described as showing so much fortitude in the face of repeated disaster). He organized his cavalry and pursued the Israelites, intending to bring them back to their slavery, or to destroy them.

But there was one final miracle against the Egyptians, for the water of the Sea of Reeds was blown back and the Israelites were able to ford it. When the pursuing Egyptians attempted to cross, however, the water came back and drowned them.

The joy of the Israelites at the final deliverance took the form of a song of triumph, after which:

> Ex.15:20. *And Miriam the prophetess, the sister of Aaron, took a timbrel in her hand; and all the women went out after her with timbrels and with dances.*

Miriam appeared earlier in the Book of Exodus as the sister who watched over the ark of the infant Moses until Pharaoh's daughter found him, but this is the first occasion on which her name is mentioned.

In aftercenturies it remained a favorite name among the Jews. In Greek and Roman times, it became "Mariamme" or "Mariamne." Two of the wives of Herod (who ruled Judea at the time of the birth of Jesus) were named Mariamne. The influence of the later spelling is to be found in the Douay Version,* where the name of the sister of Aaron and Moses is given as "Mariam."

A simplified form of "Mariamne," with the final letters omitted, is "Maria." This version may have become popular because a common Latin name was "Marius" and the feminine form of that was "Maria."

In the New Testament, there are half a dozen women bearing this version of the name. It is still Maria in many European languages, but it is "Marie" or "Marion" in French, and, of course, "Mary" in English. Most important, it is the name of Mary, the

---

* The Authorized Version is not accepted by the Catholic Church, for whom the official Bible is the Latin translation, known as the Vulgate. However, an unofficial English translation of the Old Testament was prepared by Catholic scholars in the city of Douay, France, in 1610. This is the Douay Version.

mother of Jesus. It is also the name of Mary Magdalene and of Mary of Bethany.

In the English language, "Mary" is by far the most popular feminine name because of this. It is found by itself and in common combinations such as "Mary Ann" and "Mary Jane." It also occurs in versions such as "May," "Moll," "Molly," and "Polly," all of which arise from Mary. — And it all works its way back to Miriam, the sister of Moses.

With the Sea of Reeds now behind them, the Israelites had passed beyond the boundaries of Egypt and were in the peninsula of Sinai. They were completely free of the Egyptian threat, but they now faced a largely uninhabited wilderness, incapable of supporting their huge numbers:

> Ex.15:22. *So Moses brought Israel from the Red sea, and they went out into the wilderness of Shur . . .*
>
> Ex.16:1. *And they took their journey . . . unto the wilderness of Sin . . .*

Shur and Sin are districts along the western edge of the Sinai Peninsula. Their locations are not certain but it is most commonly supposed that Shur is just east of the Sea of Reeds, while Sin (which has no connection, of course, with the English word "sin") lies to the south. The wilderness of Sin is about halfway down the length of the Sinai Peninsula; halfway to that peninsula's southern tip.

It was toward that southern tip and Mount Sinai that Moses was leading the Israelites.

# 5

## Sinai

THE ISRAELITES, facing the uninviting Sinai Peninsula after having lived in the rich delta of the Nile for so long, lost no time in complaining about the leadership of Moses and Aaron.

> Ex.16:3. . . . *Would to God we had died . . . in the land of Egypt, when we sat by the flesh pots, and when we did eat bread to the full; for ye have brought us forth into this wilderness, to kill this whole assembly with hunger.*

Facing starvation, life in Egypt, with its slavery and even with death, seemed preferable, for there they had the "flesh pots," pots in which meat was boiling or stewing.

Because of this verse, people are said "to long for the fleshpots of Egypt" whenever they want to exchange spiritual benefits for material advantages.

God, however, provided food for the hungry Israelites:

> Ex.16:13. *And it came to pass . . . in the morning . . .*
>
> Ex.16:14. . . . *behold, upon the face of the wilderness there lay a small round thing, as small as the hoarfrost on the ground.*
>
> Ex.16:15. *And when the children of Israel saw it, they said one to another, It is manna: for they wist not what it was.*

Presumably, what the Israelites said among themselves (in Hebrew, of course) was "*Man hu? Man hu?*" meaning "What is it? What is it?" This is the reason given for its being called *man* in Hebrew, a word which became "manna" in English. It is as though an English-speaking crowd were to have named the material "whatzit." (The word "wist," by the way, is an archaism meaning "knew" and the Revised Standard Version uses "knew" instead.)

Naturally, there have been attempts to identify what manna might be in the natural world by those who were not content to consider the whole thing a miracle and let it go at that. For instance, it was supposed that some tree or other plant form native to the Sinai Peninsula exuded some sort of nourishing food. The exudate of a tamarisk tree was called *mennu* by the Egyptians and some think that this was the real source of the word.

Then, there are some types of European ash trees that exude a sticky mass which is called "manna" because of these verses in the Bible. The tree itself is sometimes called the "manna tree" or the "manna ash" for that reason. A eucalyptus tree that does the same is called the "manna gum." There is even an edible lichen that is found in areas of Egypt and Arabia that is called the "manna lichen." It is quite unlikely, however, that any of these would represent the manna as described in the Bible.

However, the exudate of the manna ash has left the name firmly embedded in chemistry. The manna of the manna ash was analyzed by chemists and found to contain a sugarlike compound which was named "mannitol." The sugar it was related to was named "mannose" once that was isolated. Starchlike substances built up out of such sugars were named "mannans."

In a less material sense, manna is viewed as a kind of ideal food, fit for creatures in heaven. It is the Biblical equivalent of the nectar and ambrosia of Greek mythology. It might be used to express anything that was deeply longed for and gratefully received. The words of an eloquent speaker or the sight of home after a long absence might be like "manna from heaven."

Detailed instructions were given the Israelites as to the way in which the manna might be gathered, even to the weight to be gathered:

> Ex.16:16. . . . *Gather . . . an omer for every man . . .*

In translating a language, there is nothing much that can be done with expressions used for weights and measures, unless you know the equivalent weight or measure in your own units. Even then, the foreign units are likely to come out to an uneven number of your own units and that is inconvenient. Consequently, the world "omer" remains as in the original Hebrew. (It must have grown unfamiliar to the later Jews, for further on an omer is defined as the "tenth part of an ephah," which, of course, leaves us no better off.)

As best as can be determined now, an omer is about 7½ pints and an ephah consequently 75 pints (or 1⅙ bushels). To put it as briefly as possible, seven bushels of manna would make a day's food for sixty men.

The Israelites were instructed to gather manna only six days of the week. There was to be no gathering on the Sabbath.

> Ex.16:29. . . . *abide ye every man in his place, let no man go out of his place on the seventh day.*

In later centuries, the rabbis deduced as a general rule from this verse that journeying was to be forbidden on the Sabbath. An orthodox Jew might go as far as 2000 yards from his place but no farther. This distance has therefore entered the language as a "Sabbath journey," a phrase which can be used for any limited distance (something like the phrase "a stone's throw").

As the Israelites worked their way down the western shore of the Gulf of Suez, a new danger arose. Food had been supplied them, and later water (also by miraculous means), but now human enemies appeared. These consisted of the Amalekites (am′uh-lek-ites), a nomadic tribe who occupied southern Canaan and who conducted raids into the Sinai Peninsula:

> Ex.17:8. *Then came Amalek, and fought with Israel in Rephidim.*

As a result of this and other verses in the Bible, the word "Amalekite" is sometimes used for any marauding nomad. Moses did not take these raids calmly:

> Ex.17:9. *And Moses said unto Joshua, Choose us out men and go out, fight with Amalek: . . .*

This is the first mention of Joshua in the Bible, but from this point on he constantly serves as Moses' right-hand man in military matters. Since it was Joshua who defeated the Amalekites at Rephidim, winning Israel's first military victory, and since it was Joshua who led the Israelites forward during the conquest of Canaan after the death of Moses, his name was fairly popular among the later Jews. In the New Testament, it was given by Mary (under angelic instructions) to her Son.

The New Testament appeared in Greek, however,

and in the Greek, Joshua is written "Jesus." In fact, when Joshua of the Old Testament is mentioned in the New Testament (as he is in two places, in chapter 7, verse 45 of The Acts of the Apostles and in chapter 4, verse 8 of the Epistle to the Hebrews) he is referred to as "Jesus."

In English, we have completely lost any notion of the identity of the two names. For instance, the reverence for the name "Jesus" is such that no child of English-speaking parents is named so (although it is used freely among Spanish-speaking peoples). However, the name "Joshua" is used. Joshua Reynolds was a famous English portrait painter of the eighteenth century, and Joshua Logan is a famous American theatrical producer of the present day, just to give two examples.

The exact site of Rephidim (ref′i-dim), where the Amalekites were defeated, is not known, but tradition places it near the southern tip of the Sinai Peninsula, about 25 miles northwest of Sinai itself.

At Rephidim, Moses was visited by his father-in-law, who suggested to Moses that he delegate authority so that he himself need not attempt to decide all matters. He further urged Moses to give the Israelites a detailed code of law so that they might be able to guide their own conduct.

This leads directly to the next event, which is the climax of the Pentateuch.

The Israelites are led from Rephidim to Mount Sinai itself, the mountain on which Moses had encountered the burning bush and on which he had received his original instructions to proceed to Egypt and to assume leadership of the Israelites.

Here God made a contract (or covenant) with the Israelites, for when Moses went up the mountain alone, he was instructed to tell the Israelites that if they agreed to accept the laws given them, they would be rewarded:

> Ex.19:5. . . . *if ye will obey my voice indeed, and keep my covenant, then ye shall be a peculiar treasure unto me above all people: . . .*

The word "peculiar" comes from a Latin word meaning "private property." When God describes the Israelites as a "peculiar treasure," He means that they would be treated as His own particular possession; that they would belong to God in a particular way, more so than other groups of people. The Revised Standard Version has the phrase read, "you shall be my own possession among all peoples."

Because of this verse, the later Jews described

themselves as *am segullah*, meaning the "people of possession," which, using the original meaning of the word, can also be translated as the "peculiar people."

This phrase was also used by the early Christians to describe themselves, and also by Christian sects of modern times who felt themselves to be obeying God's laws more closely than did other people. A Christian sect founded near London in 1828 actually used "Peculiar People" as its official name.

However, when something is a private possession, it is marked off from all other similar objects. My house, for instance, is not quite like any other house, for my house belongs to me and other houses do not.

The word "peculiar" came to mean, therefore, any object that was distinctly different from all other objects of the same sort. To most people, a difference which marks one object off from all other objects of the same sort is a queer and odd difference. (Imagine if all men wore gray suits, and one man wore a scarlet one; or if all men spoke English and one man insisted on speaking only Portuguese.) Such nonconformists are peculiar and also seem queer and eccentric; so "peculiar" came to mean "queer and eccentric."

In that sense, it may be that the Jews of medieval and modern times, lost among large groups of non-

Jews but stubbornly practicing their ancient rites, are indeed a "peculiar people," but that is not the original sense of the word. And the Christian sect of Peculiar People were peculiar in that they believed in faith-healing, but that is not what they meant, either.

On the other hand, God might have selected any group of people to be his "peculiar treasure" but he selected the Israelites. In several places later in the Bible, this act of selection is referred to, and the Israelites are said to have been chosen. It is for this reason that the Jews are sometimes referred to as the "Chosen People."

In the light of later history, this choice did not seem to bring with it much material advantage, for the Jews, as a people, have had more than their share of misfortune in the more than 3000 years since the gathering at Mount Sinai.

The Israelites agreed to keep the covenant, and the beginning of God's instructions are in the form of ten general rules of conduct which, ever since, have been known as the "Ten Commandments." In Greek, these are referred to as *deka logoi* ("ten words," or, more generally, "ten statements"). From these Greek words, we get "Decalog" as a synonym for the Ten Commandments.

The Ten Commandments, in brief, are:

1) Polytheism is forbidden.

> Ex.20:3. *Thou shalt have no other gods before me.*

2) Idolatry is forbidden.

> Ex.20:4. *Thou shalt not make unto thee any graven image, or any likeness of any thing that is in heaven above, or that is in the earth beneath, or that is in the water under the earth:*
> Ex.20:5. *Thou shalt not bow down thyself to them, nor serve them: for I the Lord thy God am a jealous God . . .*

(A "graven image" is one that has been sculptured or engraved.)

The Israelites observed this commandment in later centuries and it prevented them from developing the arts of painting and sculpture. The Mohammedans adhered to it just as strictly, but used their ingenuity in indulging the natural human passion of ornamentation. Since they might not make the likeness of anything in the heavens, in the earth, or in the waters, they made abstract designs that were unlike any natural object. Mohammedans were not the only ones to do this, but since it was characteristic of Mohammedan art and since the Arabs were the original Mohammedans, such ornamentation has been referred to as "arabesque."

The Christians have been more liberal in their interpretation of this commandment, feeling that it wasn't the making of an image in itself that was forbidden, but the worshiping of such an image as a god.

However, throughout history there were always some Christian groups who favored a stricter interpretation of the second commandment. In the eighth century, a series of Byzantine emperors forbade the use of such statues and broke as many of those that existed as they could. They were the Iconoclast ("image-breaking") Emperors. Then, most of the Protestant sects favor the stricter interpretations, so that Protestant churches, in general, are bare of statues.

The word "jealous" is from the same root as "zealous." One who is zealous, is full of "zeal," full of an ardent emotion, usually with respect to doing a job that must be done. In effect, when God describes Himself as "jealous" he indicates that he is full of zeal to perform the functions of God and to do it all. He will allow none of the functions to be performed by any other entity and so he will allow no worship of other gods or of idols. One might rephrase the clause in 21:5 of the Book of Exodus as "I the Lord thy God am a God who will allow no competition."

Unfortunately, the word "jealous" has been cheapened with time. It is applied to people who are not merely intolerant of competition, but to people who are constantly suspecting competition, even when none exists. In this respect "jealousy" is considered a rather ignoble emotion, and certainly not one that is fitting for God.

Even worse, "jealousy" has been confused with the word "envy." You are "jealous" of something you possess, which you do not want to have unjustly taken over by another. You are "envious" when you want to take over, unjustly, something that is the possession of another. Thus, you are "jealous" of your own good name and fortune; you are "envious" of your neighbor's good name and fortune.

Envy is a far more ignoble emotion than jealousy and when the two are confused, the phrase, "I am a jealous God," becomes an embarrassing one.

3) Blasphemy is forbidden:

> Ex.20:7. *Thou shalt not take the name of the Lord thy God in vain . . .*

The word "vain" comes from a Latin word meaning "empty." A "vain discussion" is an empty one that achieves nothing: to do something "in vain" is to return with empty hands; to be "vain" is to have more pride in something than it deserves so that some of the pride is over nothing and is empty.

Now, as I mentioned in *Words in Genesis*, the ancient peoples attached a great deal of importance to names, and especially to names of gods. Divine names were very powerful and could only be used with proper precautions by people properly trained in their use.

Furthermore, the divine name should be used only for important purposes of religious significance. It should not be used to witness unimportant promises or, worse still, false promises. It should not be used in calling down quick curses out of casual ill-temper. It should not be used simply as an exclamation of surprise or fear or anger.

All these things are frivolous, empty of importance, and therefore "vain." To use God's name for such purposes is "to take it in vain."

4) The Sabbath is ordered kept:

> Ex.20:8. *Remember the sabbath day, to keep it holy.*

5) Respect for parents is ordered:

> Ex.20:12. *Honour thy father and thy mother . . .*

6) Murder is forbidden:

> Ex.20:13. *Thou shalt not kill.*

7) Adultery is forbidden.

> Ex.20:14. *Thou shalt not commit adultery.*

8) Theft is forbidden.

> Ex.20:15. *Thou shalt not steal.*

9) Perjury is forbidden.

> Ex.20:16. *Thou shalt not bear false witness against thy neighbour.*

10) Covetousness (that is, strong longing) for other people's possessions is forbidden.

> Ex.20:17. *Thou shalt not covet . . . any thing that is thy neighbour's.*

The Catholics count the commandments a little differently than I have given them here (which is as the Jews and Protestants count them). The Catholics consider the first two commandments as being one and divide what is given here as the tenth commandment into two. The total comes out to ten just the same.

Following the Decalog are a long series of laws, many of which apply to a society in which slavery and polygamy are permitted and which would not fit our own society without a very generous helping of Talmudic interpretation.

There are also laws involving various grades of murder, including those that are not premeditated but are done on the spur of the moment because a favorable opportunity takes place:

> Ex.21:13. *And if a man lie not in wait, but God deliver him into his hand . . .*

The picture here is of God helping the murderer by giving him his victim. This seems strange to us but it is a natural picture to anyone who believes, as the writers of the Bible did, that *all* events of every kind are ordained by God for his own purposes.

This thought gives rise to a common modern phrase. We speak of any disaster that is not caused by a particular act of some man as "an act of God." By this we include accident, sickness, flood, fire, storm, earthquake, volcanic eruptions, and all such disasters.

Then, a famous passage occurs shortly afterward:

> Ex.21:23. *And if any mischief follow, then thou shalt give life for life,*

Ex.21:24. *Eye for eye, tooth for tooth, hand for hand, foot for foot,*

Ex.21:25. *Burning for burning, wound for wound, stripe for stripe.*

This is what is known in Latin as *lex talionis* (leks tal′ee-oh′nis, "law of retaliation"). It was the purpose of the *lex talionis* in the Mosaic law not so much to enforce cruel punishments as to limit them. It established the principle that the punishment must fit the crime and not exceed it.

The law of retaliation (which should be called the law of *limited* retaliation) prevents the development of quarrels in which a slight offense results in a more severe retaliation, which brings on a still more severe one in its turn, and so on, until murder over the generations becomes commonplace. Then we have the "vendettas" of Corsica and Sicily and the "feuds" of our own Appalachian backwoods.

However, in modern times, when the advanced nations have developed decent prisons and elaborate systems of fines, the law of retaliation sounds very cruel. For that reason 12:24 of the Book of Exodus (usually misquoted as "An eye for an eye and a tooth for a tooth") has come to be a common expression, signifying a savage insistence on full revenge, without any chance of forgiveness or mercy.

Of course, provision is also made for punishment by the payment of fines in case of relatively minor offenses:

> Ex.21:32. *If the ox shall push a manservant or a maidservant; he shall give unto their master thirty shekels of silver . . .*

(where "he" refers to the owner of the ox).

The Hebrew words for coins, like those for weights and measures, are hard to translate and "shekel" is the Hebrew word itself. A shekel is a weight of silver equal to about half an ounce and its value in modern currency would be somewhere between 50 and 75 cents, so that the fine mentioned comes out to be something like $20.

The Biblical use of the word "shekel" has made it popular enough to serve as a slang expression for money even today. (Usually it is used in the plural, and humorously.)

An important verse is:

> Ex.22:18. *Thou shalt not suffer a witch to live.*

To the Israelites, any attempt to manipulate divine powers, except through God and by the proper people in the proper fashion, was wrong.

In Chapter 3, I mentioned the "wise men" of Egypt. They used their wisdom in what the Israelites considered wrong manipulation of the supernatural. Now the suffix "-ard" in English words signifies something that is done wrongly, or too much. A "coward" is one who is cowed too much. A "drunkard" is one who drinks improperly by drinking too much. Similarly, a wise man who uses his wisdom improperly is a "wise-ard" or, as we spell it today, a "wizard."

A female wizard might be referred to as a "wizardess" or a "sorceress" but is most often spoken of as a "witch."

For some reason, "witch" has always been a more fearful word than "wizard" and sometimes the word "witch" spreads out to cover both sexes. In early modern times, the searching for witches became almost a mania. Many supposed witches were executed partly on the basis of 22:18 of the Book of Exodus and partly through superstitions left over from heathen days.

A victim of the supernatural powers misused by witches was said to be "bewitched" and, in fact, "witch" and "victim" may be derived from the same ancient root-word. The art of witches is called "witchcraft" and witches were believed to hold meetings at which the devil appeared and was worshiped.

Such meetings were called "Witches' sabbath."

The best example of the witch mania, as far as Americans are concerned, took place in Salem, Massachusetts, in 1692. It should also be remembered that Joan of Arc was burnt as a witch. We disapprove of such practices now and the term "witch hunt" is used for any emotional and unjustified pursuit or persecution of some harmless group of people.

Nowadays, the fear of witches has declined to almost nothing, and yet it has not disappeared altogether. Many people still believe in such things. This belief can be found, for instance, among some of the German-speaking "Pennsylvania Dutch." The German word for "witch" is *Hexe* so that the word "to hex" has entered the English language, meaning to put under a spell.

In primitive societies, men who know the rituals designed to cast spells are called "witch doctors" because they use those spells to treat diseases. (In fact, psychiatrists who try to cure disease by doing no more than listening and talking, as though they were casting spells in their own fashion, are sometimes humorously called "witch doctors.")

Both "wizard" and "witch" have come to be used in less fearful fashion nowadays.

The word "wizard" is now applied to anyone who is particularly skillful at something, particularly in his studies. A schoolboy may be a "wiz" at mathematics, where that word is only a slang abbreviation for "wizard."

The word "witch" can be applied to any ugly old woman, whether she is suspected of magic arts or not. (The word "hag" for an ugly old woman is related to the German *Hexe*.)

Or, on the other hand, it may be applied to a nasty or troublemaking woman, even if she is young.

Strangely enough, it is even applied to a beautiful woman who is perfectly agreeable, because then her beauty seems to place you under a spell so that you are "bewitched" by her. That kind of a spell is "witchery." She is also "charming" since a charm is a kind of spell and you are "charmed" by her.

Later, among the laws handed down from Mount Sinai, there is mention of a sabbath on a yearly scale:

> Ex.23:10. *And six years thou shalt sow thy land, and shalt gather in the fruits thereof:*
>
> Ex.23:11. *But the seventh year thou shalt let it rest and lie still . . .*

This seventh year of rest for the land is like the seventh day of rest for the individual Israelite and is therefore called a "sabbatical year."

Nowadays, the expression lingers in a way that has

nothing to do with agriculture. It has been customary for many universities to give their faculty members a year's leave of absence after six years of attendance to their teaching duties. During the seventh year, they are free to do research, write scholarly books, travel for scholarly purposes, or perhaps just take the time to think. This seventh year of rest from academic duties is generally referred to as a "sabbatical."

Annual observances are also required; three of them, in fact:

> Ex.23:14. *Three times thou shalt keep a feast unto me in the year.*
>
> Ex.23:15. *Thou shalt keep the feast of unleavened bread: . . .*
>
> Ex.23:16. *And the feast of harvest . . . and the feast of ingathering . . .*

The first is, of course, Passover, while the other two are festivals of a type that are usual in agricultural societies. The "feast of harvest" was celebrated as a spring harvest at the time of the ripening of wheat. It took place seven weeks after Passover, so that it came to be called *Shabuoth* in Hebrew (the word meaning "week"), and, sometimes, the "Feast of Weeks" in English.

The actual celebration takes place on the day after the completion of seven weeks from the time of Passover; that is, the fiftieth day after Passover. This festival is mentioned in the New Testament under the Greek name of "Pentecost," which is from the Greek word for "fifty." Various Christian groups now celebrate Pentecost as the seventh Sunday after Easter (the fiftieth day, if Easter is counted as the first).

Because of the movable nature of the lunar calendar that governs the dates of Passover and Easter, the dates of Shabuoth and Pentecost vary from year to year on our own solar calender. They fall sometime between mid-May and mid-June.

The "feast of ingathering" was an autumn harvest celebrated sometime between mid-September and mid-October on our calendar. It lasted a week and was marked by the construction of small booths in the field in commemoration of the time of wandering after the Exodus, when the Israelites lived in tents and without settled homes. In Hebrew, the feast is therefore called *Sukkoth* (meaning "booths").

Another rule that leaves its mark today is:

> Ex.23:19. . . . *Thou shalt not seethe a kid in his mother's milk.*

The reason for this is not certain. It sounds as though it might be an expression of softheartedness. Having to kill a young animal for food is a shame, even though men must eat, but to boil it in the milk that was meant for its nourishment seems to be going too far.

On the other hand, it may also be that boiling young animals in milk was part of Canaanite religious practices. The Israelites might then be warned away in this fashion from idolatry, rather than from a particular way of preparing food.

However, later rabbis interpreted the verse as implying that meat products and dairy products ought not to be eaten at the same meal. Orthodox Jews avoid this even today. An orthodox Jewish family may feel it necessary to have four different sets of dishes. One would be for use only with meat-meals and a second only for dairy-meals, while the third and fourth are reserved for meat-meals and dairy-meals on Passover. (Of course, there are some articles of food such as bread, eggs and potatoes that can be eaten either with meat or dairy foods.)

When the rules laid down by God were delivered, Moses was instructed to come up the mountain and get the written version:

> Ex.24:12. . . . *I will give thee tables of stone, and a law, and commandments which I have written; that thou mayest teach them.*

Ex.24:13. *And Moses rose up, and his minister Joshua: and Moses went up into the mount of God.*

The "tables of stone" are usually pictured as a sheet of rock with straight lines bounding the sides and bottom and two semicircles bounding the top so that there are two halves, symmetrical about a vertical midline. On them are inscribed the Ten Commandments, five on one side and five on the other; or just the first ten letters of the Hebrew alphabet (which also serve as the numbers from one to ten).

Because of their association with Moses, this is referred to as the "Mosaic tablet" and is often used to symbolize Judaism. For instance, a Mosaic tablet is used as part of the insignia of Jewish chaplains in the United States armed forces.

Joshua is here referred to as "minister." The word has an interesting background. In Latin, *magis* means "more," while *minor* means "less." Therefore, if one man rules over another, the ruler is the *magister*, which has been shortened to "master" in English (though we still speak of a "magistrate," someone who has power, such as that of a judge). As for the person ruled over by the magister or master, he is the "minister" or servant.

In this case, Joshua went up the mountain as Moses' servant or assistant. He was Moses' minister.

As time went on, however, the word "minister" gained in importance. Thus, the king's ministers may have been servants to him, but, in his name, they ruled other people. High government officials, with definite areas of responsibility, are ministers and the area in their charge is a "ministry." The highest of the ministers, as in Great Britain, becomes a "Prime Minister" ("first servant"). In Great Britain, where the monarch is a figurehead, and does not take any actual part in the government, the "first servant" is actually the ruler or master of the nation. The minister has become the magister.

Again, anyone who assists at religious services is a minister, but, of course, it is no disgrace to be in the service of God. Rather, it is an honor. After the time of the Reformation, those Protestants who conducted the services called themselves ministers rather than priests and that custom is still with us today.

God next proceeded to give Moses detailed instructions as to the construction of several supremely sacred objects. The Israelites were expected to spare no expense and effort in expressing their feelings toward God. Gold, silver, and precious stones were used in profusion:

> Ex.25:7. *Onyx stones, and stones to be set in the ephod, and in the breastplate.*

The "ephod" is an article of clothing for the priest, made of white linen for ordinary priests but highly ornamented for the high priest. A "breastplate" is usually an article of armor. Here, however, it is a garment to be worn over the ephod. The Revised Standard Version uses the word "breastpiece" instead.

Instructions continue:

> Ex.25:8. *And let them make me a sanctuary; that I may dwell among them.*
>
> Ex.25:9. *According to all that I shew thee, after the pattern of the tabernacle, and the pattern of all the instruments thereof, even so shall ye make it.*
>
> Ex.25:10. *And they shall make an ark of shittim wood: two cubits and a half shall be the length thereof, and a cubit and a half the breadth thereof, and a cubit and a half the height thereof.*

The word "sanctuary" means a holy place. It comes from a Latin word meaning "holy" (and so do such related words as "sanctity," "sanctify," "saint," and so on, as I described in *Words in Genesis*).

Holy places were places of refuge, not only among the Israelites, but among most peoples. The feeling seems to be that a person who has fled for safety to some temple, shrine, or altar is under the protection of the god to which those places are dedicated. To drag such a person away is to insult the god and commit blasphemy.

For that reason, "sanctuary" has come to mean any refuge or place of safety, even when holiness is not involved in the slightest. Nowadays, in fact, the word is most commonly used in phrases such as "bird sanctuary" or "game sanctuary" to cover areas where birds or beasts find themselves safe from man and his weapons.

The sanctuary was not a large structure. Allowing eighteen inches to a cubit (which comes from the Latin word for "elbow" and represents the distance from elbow to fingertip), it was a little less than four feet long, and little over two feet wide and high. It is the third and final "ark" of the Bible and, like the others, it is an enclosure protecting something.

The first ark, Noah's, enclosed and protected many men and animals; the second ark, Moses', enclosed and protected an infant. This third ark enclosed and protected the evidence of the covenant between God and the Israelites at Mount Sinai. The evidence, or testimony, consisted of the Mosaic tablets brought down from Sinai by Moses. For this reason, this ark was called "the Ark of the Testimony" or "the Ark of the Covenant."

The Ark of the Covenant was to be enclosed in a "tabernacle," a wooden structure of two rooms, covered with curtains. The word itself is from a Latin expression meaning "a small room" and, as a matter of fact, the word "tavern" comes from the same root.

The booths constructed by the Jews at the time of Sukkoth (which I mentioned earlier in the chapter) are examples of small rooms and, in English, Sukkoth is referred to as the "Feast of Tabernacles."

However, because of the particular tabernacle that housed the very holy Ark of the Covenant, the word came to mean more than just a small room. It came almost to be synonymous with "church" or "temple." Strangely enough, it came to be applied to Protestant places of worship that contained a particularly large room. Tents or other structures that contain large auditoriums where crowds might gather for evangelical meetings are called tabernacles.

In particular, the Tabernacle (with a capital letter) applies to a structure built by the Mormons in 1867 in Salt Lake City. It has a dome seventy feet high held up by a latticework of wood.

The Ark of the Covenant contained ornamentation on the outside:

> Ex.25:17. *And thou shalt make a mercy seat of pure gold . . .*
>
> Ex.25:18. *And thou shalt make two cherubims of gold . . . in the two ends of the mercy seat.*

The mercy seat was a plate of gold on top of the Ark and it played a part in the ritual that was to ask pardon of God for the sins of the people. He was to show them mercy (it was hoped) and hence the name.

The Israelites later felt that the very presence of God hovered over the mercy seat between the two cherubims; that this was his dwelling place. The presence of God was referred to as the *Shekinah*, a Hebrew word meaning "dwelling."

As for the "cherubims," they are not described except in the statement a couple of verses later that they have wings. (I discussed this word in *Words in Genesis.*)

In addition to the ark, two other objects were placed within the tabernacle:

> Ex.25:23. *Thou shalt also make a table . . .*
>
> Ex.25:30. *And thou shalt set upon the table* shewbread . . .
>
> Ex.25:31. *And thou shalt make a candlestick of pure gold: . . .*
>
> Ex.25:32. *And six branches shall come out*

*of the sides of it; three . . . out of the one side, and three . . . out of the other side.*

"Shewbread" would be spelled "showbread" in American usage. The Authorized Version conforms to the spelling rules in England so that "favor" is spelled "favour" and "color" is spelled "colour." I will use American spelling except when actually quoting a verse from the Bible.

The showbread consisted of twelve pieces of unleavened bread intended to be placed on display as an indication (according to later interpretation) that the material things of the world were the gift of God; and as gratitude for all, like bread, that made life possible. Because the bread was brought into the presence of God, it could be called "bread of the Presence" and, in fact, the Revised Standard Version uses that phrase here. The Hebrew term for showbread is *Lekhem happanim*, or "bread of faces," meaning bread that was brought before the face of God.

The candlestick (called "lampstand" in the Revised Standard Version) can hold seven little clay lamps. The exact shape of the candlestick, with its central holder and three branches on either side, is so familiar in connection with synagogue worship, that, like the Mosaic tablets, it has come to be used as a symbol of Judaism.

Once the instructions for the tabernacle and its contents are completed, attention turns to the priests that are to serve at the tabernacle:

> Ex.28:1. *And take thou unto thee Aaron thy brother and his sons with him . . . that he may minister unto me in the priest's office . . .*

This establishes the priesthood in Aaron's family, so that one can speak of the "Aaronic priesthood."

The clothing to be worn by the high priest is described in lavish detail:

> Ex.28:4. *And these are the garments which they shall make; a breastplate, and an ephod, and a robe, and a broidered coat, a mitre, and a girdle: . . .*

The word "mitre" (or "miter" in the American spelling) comes from the Greek *mitra,* which was a narrow band worn about the head and designed to keep the hair in place. Young women today sometimes wear such a band. In Roman times it came to be applied to more elaborate headdresses.

The Hebrew word used here refers to something which is far nearer what we would today call a "turban," and, in fact, the word is translated "turban" in the Revised Standard Version.

In the Catholic Church and in some other Christian

sects, the bishops wear special conical headdresses with two peaks and these are called "miters," in reference to the Aaronic headdress. The two peaks have come to be associated with the miter in the minds of men now. Thus, the valve separating the left auricle of the heart from the left ventricle consists of two flaps of tissue which, when closed, belly upward into twin peaks. This is therefore called the mitral valve.

The high priest's attire includes two mysterious objects:

> Ex.28:30. *And thou shalt put in the breastplate of judgment the Urim and the Thummim; and they shall be upon Aaron's heart, when he goeth in before the Lord . . .*

Exactly what the Urim (yoo′rim) and Thummim (thum′im) were, no one knows and the Hebrew words (which mean "lights and perfection") give no hint. Later mentions of them in the Bible seem to show they were used as divining instruments to learn the will of God, but their use dropped out early in the history of Israel.

They turned up again in modern American history, however, in connection with the Mormons. Mormonism began when a young American farmer, Joseph Smith, reported in 1827 that an angel had given him a book of golden sheets on which strange markings were to be found. He translated these into what is now called the "Book of Mormon," a supposed history of certain Jews who had fled Jerusalem before it was captured by the Babylonians in the sixth century B.C. and who somehow made their way to North America.

Smith explained that he had translated the strange language upon the golden sheets by means of the Urim and Thummim. These had been given him by the angel and, using them as spectacles, he could read the writing as English.

God's instructions continue, and while Moses was on Sinai, the Israelites below were growing impatient. Thinking that Moses was dead, they demanded that Aaron make them new gods. For this purpose, Aaron collected the gold ornaments of the people:

> Ex.32:4. *And he . . . made . . . a molten calf: and they said, These be thy gods, O Israel, which brought thee up out of the land of Egypt.*

Aaron then built an altar and the people proceeded to worship the calf (or young bull). This is not as queer as it sounds, for the bull was one of the sacred animals of Egypt, so that the Israelites had had ample opportunity to observe bull-worship. In fact, later on in their history, bull-worship was to crop up again.

What seems to have impressed people who read this passage, however, is not so much the calf itself as the fact that it was made out of gold. For this reason, the expression "golden calf" has come to be a contemptuous term for money. To "worship the golden calf" means to allow money and money-making to become the most important thing in life.

God is, naturally, displeased at the worship of the golden calf, and orders Moses back down the mountain:

> Ex.32:9. *And the Lord said unto Moses, I have seen this people, and, behold, it is a stiffnecked people:*

The image is that of an animal which holds its neck stiff and moves straight ahead, refusing to allow its head to be turned to one side so that it might move out of its path. "Stiffnecked" thus has come to mean "stubborn" and because of its use in this verse, it refers particularly to stubbornness in doing evil.

Moses, however, pleaded on behalf of the Israelites and averted their destruction. He and Joshua then descended the mountain and were in their turn angry when they saw the details of what was happening. Moses broke the tablets of the law and then had a number of the more guilty killed.

After that, he went back up the mountain, where new tablets were made. This time he returned to find the people patiently waiting:

> Ex.34:30. *And when Aaron and all the children of Israel saw Moses, behold, the skin of his face shone; and they were afraid to come nigh him.*

The Hebrew words stating that the skin of Moses' face shone could be translated to the effect that the skin sent out "beams of light." The Latin words of the Vulgate used here mean "horns of light." For that reason, Moses was sometimes pictured as having horns. Michelangelo's majestic statue of Moses shows him with horns!

With Moses returned, the tabernacle and all else was built and made exactly according to instructions.

And with that, the Book of Exodus ends.

# 6

## Aaron

THE THIRD BOOK of the Bible is devoted very largely to rules and instructions guiding the behavior of the priests and detailing the sacrifices which they were to conduct.

The Alexandrian Jews named the book *Levitikon*

("concerning the Levites," that is, the priests) when they translated the Bible into Greek. In Latin, the name became *Leviticus* (lee-vit′ih-kus) and that is the name still used in the various English translations. I shall use the abbreviation "Lev." to indicate verses from this book.

The Hebrew name of the book, as is usual for the books of Moses, is named for the first words. The initial verse begins:

> Lev.1:1. *And the Lord called unto Moses . . .*

Consequently the Hebrew name is *Vayyikra* ("He called").

The first chapter deals with burnt offerings, or sacrifices of domestic animals that are killed and then burned according to a fixed rite. The second chapter deals with the offerings of plant products. Thus:

> Lev.2:4. *And if thou bring an oblation of a meat offering baken in the oven, it shall be unleavened cakes of fine flour mingled with oil, or unleavened wafers anointed with oil.*

The word "oblation" is the translation of a Hebrew word, *korban*, meaning "something brought near"; near to God, that is, as an offering. "Oblation" is from Latin words meaning "to bring forward"; in order, that is, to offer it. "Oblation" could, strictly speaking, be used for anything offered to God, but it has been confined mostly to plant products. The Revised Standard Version uses "offering" in place of "oblation."

The expression "meat offering" used in this chapter seems to make it an animal product, for meat, nowadays, is used almost exclusively to mean animal muscle. An older meaning for "meat," however, is "food in general." We speak of "meat and drink," for instance, when we mean "food and drink."

The Revised Standard Version removes the possibility of confusion by calling it a "cereal-offering."

Finally, the book turns to Aaron, who is formally installed as high priest by Moses.

> Lev.8:12. *And he poured of the anointing oil upon Aaron's head, and anointed him, to sanctify him.*

In ancient days, soap was unknown, and a common way of cleaning the body was to rub it down with oil, particularly perfumed oil. For this reason, anointing a person — that is, pouring oil upon him — was associated with purification, with washing away spiritual sin, and making him fit for a holy office.

The anointment of Aaron for the high priesthood set an example. In later centuries, when the Israelites established a kingdom, the king was anointed, too. This is carried on to this day among Christian nations.

Because it was the anointing, along with the religious ceremonies, that made a man a king, the Israelites commonly referred to the king as "the Anointed one," or "the Lord's Anointed."

The word "anoint" comes by a rather complicated route from the Latin *unguere*, meaning "to oil." Any oily or greasy material which is applied to the skin can therefore be said to be an "ointment" or an "unguent" or an "unction."

In one of the Roman Catholic sacraments, a person in danger of death, who is at the end, or the extremity, of his life, is anointed with holy oil with accompanying prayer. This is called "extreme unction."

The installation of Aaron proceeds with numerous other rituals, and the importance of following ritual exactly is then shown. Nadab and Abihu, the two oldest sons of Aaron, burn incense at the altar according to the wrong ritual. (In what way it was wrong is not actually described.) They are destroyed as a result and the priesthood then descends through Aaron's third son, Eleazar.

The Israelites are then instructed in those animals that are "clean" — that is, which may be eaten and sacrified — and those which are "unclean."

All societies have their special habits of diet which sometimes may not seem particularly reasonable. For instance, Americans will usually refuse to eat horse-meat or dog-meat or cat-meat, though people of other nationalities will.

The Israelite food habits were made part of ritual:

> Lev.11:3. *Whatsoever parteth the hoof, and is clovenfooted, and cheweth the cud, among the beasts, that shall ye eat.*

This includes cattle, sheep, and goats. As an example of an animal that doesn't qualify:

> Lev.11:7. *And the swine, though he divide the hoof, and be clovenfooted, yet he cheweth not the cud; he is unclean to you.*
>
> Lev.11:8 *Of their flesh shall ye not eat . . .*

It is because of these instructions that Jews have, throughout history, refused to eat pork and pork products.

The Hebrew word *kosher* means "fit" or "proper" and is applied to food that is fit and proper to eat according to these "dietary laws." Thus, pork is not kosher under any circumstances. Beef can be kosher if it is prepared according to proper rituals.

The word has even been adopted into American slang, usually in the negative. Something "isn't kosher" if there seems something wrong with it.

For the Christians, the Mosaic dietary laws fell out of use. Since pork and pork products make excellent eating and since pork is usually cheaper than beef, it is a favorite article of diet among Christians. The fact that Jews (if orthodox) don't eat pork has always been very noticeable, therefore, and it hides the fact that swine are by no means the only unclean animals.

The Bible particularly mentions the camel and the hare as unclean. Other mammals, though not specifically mentioned in this connection, are clearly unclean. The horse has a single hoof on each foot so he is not "cloven-footed" and is unclean. Dogs and cats have no hoofs at all and so are unclean.

The instructions go on:

> Lev.11:9. *These shall ye eat of all that are in the waters: whatsoever hath fins and scales . . . them shall ye eat.*

From this, it follows that shellfish, such as oysters, crabs, clams, and lobsters, as well as sea mammals such as seals and whales, all lacking fins and scales, are unclean.

Unclean birds are listed; and strangely enough, four types of insects that *are* clean, varieties of locusts and grasshoppers, are listed.

After several chapters detailing the matter of cleanness and uncleanness in connection with childbirth and disease, something comes up which has left an interesting mark on the English language.

Once a year, it seems, the sins of the Israelites must be taken care of, and the responsibility falls on the high priest:

> Lev.16:7. . . . *he shall take . . . two goats, and present them before the Lord at the door of the tabernacle . . .*
>
> Lev.16:8. *And Aaron shall cast lots upon the two goats; one lot for the Lord, and the other lot for the scapegoat.*
>
> Lev.16:9. *And Aaron shall bring the goat upon which the Lord's lot fell, and offer him for a sin offering.*
>
> Lev.16:10. *But the goat, on which the lot fell to be the scapegoat, shall be presented alive before the Lord, to make an atonement with him, and to let him go for a scapegoat into the wilderness.*
>
> . . . . .
>
> Lev.16:21. *And Aaron shall lay both his hands upon . . . the live goat, and confess over him all the iniquities of the children of Israel . . . putting them upon the head of the goat . . .*

Lev.16:22. *And the goat shall bear upon him all their iniquities unto a land not inhabited: . . .*

The prefix "scape-" is a form of the word "escape" so that the "scapegoat" is the "goat that escaped" into the wilderness. The sins of the people had been transferred to the goat in this rite so that any punishment that was the consequence of those sins would fall upon the scapegoat and not upon the people.

For this reason, the word has come to mean any person or group of people who are made to suffer punishment when the real guilty ones can't be reached. The Jews themselves suffered horribly as scapegoats under Nazi rule in Germany, when the Germans, unable for a time to turn upon the nations that had defeated them in World War I, made do with the defenseless Jews in their midst.

The Hebrew word which is translated in the Authorized Version as "scapegoat" is *Azazel* (uh-zay′zel), and the Revised Standard Version uses "Azazel" instead of "scapegoat." Thus, in 16:8 of the Book of Leviticus, what is being said is that one of the goats is chosen for God and the other for Azazel.

No one is certain what exactly Azazel means, but the best guess seems to be that it is the name of a demon of the wilderness who was considered to oppose God and be the source of sin. The goat being sent into the wilderness is thus sent back to the demon, Azazel, and the load of sin it carries returns to the starting point.

In the apocryphal book of Enoch (which I mentioned in *Words in Genesis*) there is a long account about a rebellion of angels against God at the time of the creation of man. Azazel was supposed to be the head of those rebelling angels, and although he was defeated and cast into Hell, he remained the chief opponent of God and the source of all sin.

Later legends substituted other names for Azazel as that of the leader of the rebellious angels. In *Paradise Lost*, Milton, in dealing with the story of Adam and Eve, makes Azazel one of the more important of the rebellious angels, but not the leader.

The Mohammedans have their version also. After the defeat of the rebellious angels, the name of the leader, Azazel, is changed to "Eblis," who becomes the chief of the demons. This name is probably derived from the Greek *diabolis*, as our own word "devil" is. Eblis is thus the Mohammedan Devil in actual name.

The use of the word "devil" follows quickly, when the Israelites are once again warned against worshiping the false gods of other peoples:

> Lev.17:7. *And they shall no more offer their sacrifices unto devils . . .*

The Revised Standard Version changes the word "devils" into "satyrs." The satyrs were legendary demigods of the Greeks. They were pictured as being goats below the waist and men above, except that they had goat horns upon their heads. They were supposed to live in the forest where they led gay and immoral lives. They represented the multiplying powers of animals, so that they were fertility gods.

The peoples surrounding the Israelites had similar fertility gods and when any of these peoples (and the Greeks, too) held festivals in honor of satyrs, or satyr-like beings, that festival was apt to be marked by immoral practices. The Israelites disapproved of such practices and were certain that these satyrs were nothing but demons, and very evil ones at that.

This remains with us, too. Neither Jews nor Christians, these days, actually believe there are satyrs in the woods. However, the picture of the devil that is usually drawn, even today, is that of a man with horns on his head, with a cloven hoof like that of a goat, and with a tail. The Devil, in other words, is still pictured as a satyr.

In this respect, a particular god is mentioned by name:

> Lev.18:21. *And thou shalt not let any of thy seed pass through the fire to Molech, neither shalt thou profane the name of thy God: . . .*

Molech, or Moloch (moh′lok), was the chief god of some of the Canaanite peoples and indeed the name comes from a Semitic word for "king." What made the worship of Moloch so horrible was that it involved human sacrifice; in particular, the sacrifice of children. It seems hard to believe that people could do such things, but in times of great trouble, it was easy to believe that the dearer the sacrifice, the more apt the gods were to help you.

As a result of this, the word "Moloch" is used today to represent anything that demands the sacrifice of the dearest. War, for instance, can be described as a Moloch that demands human sacrifice.

The Israelites in later years were often tempted to worship Moloch or some of the other gods worshiped by surrounding nations. In doing so, they would have violated God's solemn commandments and, as is said in this verse, "profaned" the name of God.

"Profane" comes from Latin words meaning "before the temple," that is, not within the temple and therefore not holy. One profanes any holy thing by acting as though it were not holy. By violating God's commandment, one acts as though the commandment were not holy and thus profanes God.

To use the name of God for trifling reasons or for sinful reasons is to profane it. For that reason, bad language is called "profanity."

"Profane" does not necessarily have to be a word of disapproval. It can be used simply to mean things that are not holy and reserved for God, but are worldly and reserved for ordinary uses. For that reason, to speak of "the sacred and profane" is a way of saying "everything."

A variety of other practices are forbidden. For instance:

> Lev.19:31. *Regard not them that have familiar spirits . . .*

Again, this is a prohibition against any form of witchcraft or wizardry. A witch or wizard can make use of the spirits of the dead or of demons to divine the future. The spirit consulted by the witch or wizard must answer because the proper spells are used. The spirit is therefore a kind of servant, or even slave, to its human master or mistress. The Latin word for servant is *famulus*, so such a "servant-spirit" is a "familiar spirit."

Of course, people are informal with their servants and do not use respectful forms of address. For that reason, "familiar" has come to mean "to be on friendly and informal terms with." Thus, parents, their children, and other relatives, all on informal, friendly terms with one another, are called a "family." Because of this, a "familiar spirit" sounds to modern ears like a "friendly spirit." That, however, is not the point. Even a very unfriendly spirit can be a "familiar" if you have the right spells — at least in the view of peoples in earlier times who believed in such things.

The Revised Standard Version has the verse read, "Do not turn to mediums . . ." "Medium" comes from a Latin word meaning "middle." A person who consults the spirits of the dead stands in the middle between the dead and the living and is therefore a medium.

Eventually, the Book of Leviticus turns to the matter of festivals. Two are mentioned in detail:

> Lev.23:24. . . . *In the seventh month, in the first day of the month, shall ye have a sabbath, a memorial of blowing of trumpets . . .*
>
> Lev.23:27. *Also on the tenth day of this seventh month, there shall be a day of atonement: . . . and ye shall afflict your souls . . .*

The seventh month is Tishri. It is the time of the autumn harvest and the autumnal equinox. Like Nisan (the time of Passover and the vernal equinox), Tishri is a natural place to start a new year. In fact, the two holidays here mentioned grew particularly holy and helped fix Tishri as the first month of the year among the Jews.

Tishri is considered the beginning of the year in the Jewish calendar and the festival referred to in 23:24 of the Book of Leviticus as taking place on the first day of this month is popularly called the "Jewish New Year." It falls some time in September or, occasionally, in very early October.

The Hebrew name for the festival is *Rosh Hashonah*, meaning "head of the year"; in other words, the beginning of the year. The trumpet referred to is a ram's horn, called *shofar* in Hebrew. Its sound is the high point of the celebration.

Ten days after Rosh Hashonah is the "Day of Atonement" referred to in chapter 23, verse 27 of the Book of Leviticus. This falls in late September or early October. The Hebrew name is *Yom Kippur* (of which "Day of Atonement" is a direct translation). On that day, Jews observe a complete fast; that is, they "afflict their soul."

Rosh Hashonah and Yom Kippur taken together are often referred to as the "high holidays," the word "high" here meaning "great" or "important."

The word "atonement," by the way, is used for the removal of sin by any method. Sin is viewed as separating a man from God, so when sin is removed, it is possible for a man to approach God once more and be "at one" with him again. By running "at one" into the single word "atone," the pronunciation is changed and the derivation is hidden. The word "atone" is now usually used to mean a making up for some action that has brought misery or harm.

As in the Book of Exodus, a sabbatical year — a seventh year in which the land is allowed to remain fallow — is ordained. Now, however, it is followed by something further. After seven sabbatical years, forty-nine years altogether, there is a kind of super-sabbatical year:

> Lev.25:9. *Then shalt thou cause the trumpet of the jubilee to sound . . . in the day of atonement . . .*
>
> Lev.25:10. *And ye shall hallow the fiftieth year, and proclaim liberty throughout all the land unto all the inhabitants thereof: it shall be a jubilee unto you; and ye shall return every man unto his possession, and ye shall return every man unto his family.*

The word "jubilee" is derived from the Hebrew word *yobel,* which is the trumpet with which the fiftieth year opens. The phrase "trumpet of the jubilee" sounds as though it means "trumpet of the trumpet" therefore, and the Revised Standard Version substitutes "loud trumpet" for the phrase.

Since it comes every fifty years, a jubilee has come to be any celebration of a fiftieth anniversary, especially if it is a joyful occasion. In 1617, for instance, a "Protestant Jubilee" was held in Germany to celebrate the hundredth anniversary (two fifties) of the year in which Martin Luther nailed his ninety-five theses to the church door and began the Reformation. In 1769, a "Shakespeare Jubilee" was held at Stratford-on-Avon to celebrate the two hundredth (four fifties) anniversary of Shakespeare's birth.

Sometimes the fiftieth anniversary of the beginning of a reign is marked as a jubilee. George III of England celebrated one in 1809 as he was beginning his fiftieth year as ruler. Queen Victoria celebrated one in 1887 after she had reigned a full fifty years.

It has gotten so, however, that "jubilee" is becoming synonymous with anniversary, and different kinds are celebrated. For instance, in 1897, Queen Victoria had reigned sixty years and she therefore celebrated her "Diamond Jubilee." Then, in 1935, George V of England, having reigned for twenty-five years, celebrated his "Silver Jubilee." This, however, loses the real meaning of the term.

In the Catholic Church, a year is sometimes set aside as a "Holy Year" for one purpose or another and this is called a Jubilee. The first such Jubilee was declared by Pope Boniface VIII in 1300. Such Jubilees are now usually declared at intervals of twenty-five years but they can be declared at any time that the Pope sees fit.

There is an apocryphal book* called Book of the Jubilees. It consists of the material of the Book of Genesis and the first part of the Book of Exodus, with various legends added and inserted. It gets its name because it divided the events it describes into units of forty-nine years, from Jubilee to Jubilee, in other words.

During the year of the Jubilee, according to the Biblical directions, all land which had been sold reverted to its ancestral owners, and all slaves were freed. If such rules were followed, this year would be a happy one to many people, and one would suppose that words like "jubilant" and "jubilation," which signify a state of joy, with people shouting and laughing, ought to come from "jubilee." However, these words do not. They come from the Latin *jubilum*, meaning "a wild shout," and the similarity is pure coincidence.

Chapter 25, verse 10 of the Book of Leviticus has an interesting connection with American history.

---

* This is a book that is written in the style of the books of the Bible and is similar in subject matter, but is not considered inspired by God and is therefore not included in the Bible. I discuss this a bit in *Words in Genesis.*

The phrase "proclaim liberty throughout all the land unto all the inhabitants thereof" refers to the slaves that were set free at the sound of the trumpet that began the year of Jubilee. This same phrase was engraved on a bell that was cast in England in 1735 and then shipped to Philadelphia. Because of the Biblical verse upon it, it was known as the "Liberty Bell."

In 1776, it rang out to announce the signing of the Declaration of Independence, and this gave a new and literal meaning to its name. It was a defective bell, however, that had to be twice recast while it was being manufactured because of the brittleness of the alloy that was being used. In 1835, while tolling for the death of John Marshall, fourth (and greatest) Chief Justice of the Supreme Court, it finally cracked. The cracked Liberty Bell, with the Biblical quotation upon it, is now one of the most revered symbols of American ideals.

The Book of Leviticus approaches its end by offering the Israelites great reward in terms of peace and prosperity if they obey the rules of conduct given them. On the other hand, if they ignore the rules, they will suffer famine and defeat in war. At one point, famine is referred to as follows:

> Lev.26:26. *And when I have broken the staff of your bread . . .*

It is food that supports life, as a staff supports a man, and "bread" (like "meat," which I mentioned earlier) can be used for food in general, as in the familiar phrase "Give us this day our daily bread." However, among poor people through much of the history of the world, meat was a rare delicacy, and grain of one sort or another made up most of the diet. Food *was* mostly bread.

For that reason, this verse and a few others in the Bible like it, has given rise to the well-known saying, "Bread is the staff of life."

The last verses of the book deal with objects "devoted" to God. Thus:

> Lev.27:29. *None devoted, which shall be devoted of men, shall be redeemed; but shall surely be put to death.*

The word "devote" comes from a Latin word meaning "to vow." Something that is devoted is given to God through a solemn vow and, thereafter, it cannot be used for private purposes. It must be burned, or, if it can't be burned, it must be stored in the temple. If it is an animal, it must be sacrificed.

In primitive times, an entire town being besieged might be "devoted" in case of victory, and then all the men would be killed, while women and children were sold into slavery. For that reason "devoted" can be used to mean "doomed."

The word has come to be used in a more general way. To dedicate oneself to the service of anyone or anything is to be devoted. A mother may be devoted to her children, or a man may be devoted to his job. In particular, a man who is devoted to the ways of religion (not in the old sense of being marked for death, but in the sense of giving himself over completely) is "devout."

And, as the Book of Leviticus ends, the stay at Sinai approaches its end. The Israelites must now make ready to travel toward Canaan.

# 7

## Paran

In preparation for leaving Mount Sinai, a preliminary organization must take place. This includes a census, or a numbering of all the males who are twenty years old or more and are thus potential warriors. Another numbering is included later in the book, when Canaan is approached.

Because of these numberings, the Alexandrian Jews, when they translated the Bible into Greek, called the book *Arithmoi* ("numbers"). When the Bible was translated into Latin, the name of the book was changed to *Numeri.* Then, when it was translated into English, the Latin name was, for once, translated also, into "Numbers." I shall use the abbreviation "Num." to indicate verses from this book.

The Hebrew name is taken from the first verse, which begins:

> Num.1:1. *And the Lord spake unto Moses in the wilderness of Sinai . . .*

so that it is *Bemidbar* ("in the wilderness"). This happens to be a good title because the action does take place in the wilderness between Sinai and Canaan.

As a preliminary to the account of the first census, the names of the leaders of each tribe are given. None of them play any further part in the Biblical story, but the names are carefully preserved anyway, because the Israelites, like most people everywhere and throughout time, were fascinated by genealogies and loved to trace back their family histories. With the list of leaders complete, the Bible says:

> Num.1:16. *These were the renowned of the congregation, princes of the tribes of their fathers . . .*

To modern ears, this sounds as though the tribes were monarchies and that royalty was involved. Actually, "prince" is from the Latin *princeps*, meaning "to take first place," and can be applied to a leader in any field, royalty or not. We speak of a "merchant prince," for instance, meaning an important merchant.

The Revised Standard Version avoids this touch of apparent royalty by translating the phrase in 1:16 of the Book of Numbers, "the leaders of their ancestral tribes."

The number of warriors of each tribe is given and they are reported as follows:

| | |
|---|---|
| Reuben | 46,500 |
| Simeon | 59,300 |
| Gad | 45,650 |
| Judah | 74,600 |
| Issachar | 54,400 |
| Zebulun | 57,400 |
| Ephraim | 40,500 |
| Manasseh | 32,200 |
| Benjamin | 35,400 |
| Dan | 62,700 |
| Asher | 41,500 |
| Naphtali | 53,400 |
| TOTAL | 603,550 |

The tribe of Levi is not listed at this point because it is reserved for the priesthood and not for warfare. Nevertheless, there are twelve tribes in the list. The reason for this is that Jacob's eleventh son, Joseph, is represented by two tribes, Ephraim and Manasseh, traditionally descended from the two sons of Joseph.

The numbers of the tribe of Judah, by the way, are given thus:

> Num.1:27. *Those that were numbered of . . . the tribe of Judah, were threescore and fourteen thousand and six hundred.*

It was an old-fashioned habit among the English (and among other peoples, too) to count by twenties. The reason we count by tens, you see, is that we have ten fingers. In the day when most people went barefoot, or wore open-toed sandals, it was easy to bring the toes in as well, and to work out more difficult sums in that way. Using both fingers and toes, one would get into the habit of counting by twenties.

The next step beyond counting on fingers and toes was to make notches on a piece of wood. Because of the importance attached to twenty by that time, a specially large mark was made to stand for every twentieth count. "Score" is from an old Anglo-Saxon word for such a mark (which is why we "keep score" when we are counting something) and it came to be used for the number twenty.

Thus, "threescore" is, actually, three twenties, or sixty. "Threescore and fourteen" is sixty plus fourteen, or seventy-four. The Revised Standard Version eliminates this old-fashioned form of counting and has the verse read "the number of the tribe of Judah was seventy-four thousand six hundred."

Nevertheless, partly because of its use in the Bible, counting by scores has a stately and important sound about it. Thus, Lincoln began his Gettysburg Address with a reference to the time, eighty-seven years before, when the United States had been founded. He started his address "Fourscore and seven years ago — " showing at once that he was going to give a speech of Biblical solemnity. The effect would have been killed if he had started, "Eighty-seven years ago — "

After the census, Moses is directed to arrange the tribes in a square about the Ark of the Covenant and the tabernacle that housed it, each tribe in a fixed place. The Levites were to march with the tabernacle itself at the center, each clan of the tribe in charge of a particular part of the furnishings.

The Levites are then numbered separately and the number of males (including children) is 22,000. This makes them by far the smallest tribe.

After that follows further instructions and laws. For instance, the procedure of testing a woman who is accused of a crime is described. This involves putting the woman under a curse that will harm her if she is guilty but will leave her unharmed if she is innocent. This isn't our modern way of doing things, but in a society which believes in the power of curses, it could work. If a woman knew she was guilty and believed the curse would therefore make her fall sick, she might indeed fall sick and be forced to confess her guilt. If she knew she was innocent, she would be confident the curse would not harm her, and it would not.

This method of testing guilt or innocence is called "trial by ordeal." Ordeal comes from an old Teutonic word meaning "judgment." (The German word for judgment is *Urteil.*) Because such trials usually mean placing the accused person in some uncomfortable or even painful position (which was supposed not to harm him if he were innocent), "ordeal" has come to mean any trying or difficult experience.

In the description of this particular trial by ordeal, part of the procedure is described as follows:

> Num.5:17. *And the priest shall take holy water in an earthen vessel . . .*

By "holy water" is meant water which is reserved

for use in connection with religious ritual. This is a common expression now, because holy water (blessed by a priest) is used for numerous rites in the Catholic Church.

The actual curse is given and the woman must accept it:

> Num.5:22. . . . *And the woman shall say, Amen, amen.*

"Amen" is a Hebrew word meaning "truly." By saying it in response to someone else's statement, you grant the truth of the statement and share in the responsibility of making it. It is then like saying "So be it."

In this case, the woman, by saying "amen," accepts the curse and joins in making it. She agrees to have it fall on herself in case she is guilty.

Naturally, the word is also used when a prayer is offered up to God for something that is desired by the congregation. Since most hymns express a hope that God be properly glorified or that men be saved from evil and misfortune, it is common to end them with an "amen."

Because of all this, the Hebrew word has become a familiar part of the English language and is sometimes used simply as an expression of hearty agreement, as in the phrase "Amen to that."

Special rules are given a little later for the conduct of those people who wished to separate themselves from worldly affairs and dedicate themselves to the service of God:

> Num.6:2. . . . *When either man or woman shall separate themselves to vow a vow of a Nazarite . . .*
>
> Num.6:3. *He shall separate himself from wine and strong drink . . .*
>
> Num.6:5. *All the days of the vow of his separation there shall no razor come upon his head . . .*

"Nazarite" comes from a Hebrew word meaning "to separate." The vow was usually taken for limited times, but there are three cases in the Bible of a vow for life. The most famous is the case of Samson, in whose life the matter of forbidding the hair to be cut is crucial. Then there is Samuel and, in the New Testament, John the Baptist seems to have been a Nazarite.

The leaders of the various tribes then brought identical offerings to the sanctuary, Passover was celebrated (it was now a year since the Exodus), and the Israelites began their march toward Canaan.

> Num.10:12. *And the children of Israel took their journeys out of the wilderness of Sinai; and . . . rested in the wilderness of Paran.*

The wilderness of Paran (pay′ran) is at the northern end of the Gulf of Akaba. In other words, the distance covered is rather more than half that from Sinai to Canaan. (The wilderness of Paran was mentioned in the Book of Genesis. It was there that Ishmael and his mother went to live after they left the household of Abraham; see *Words in Genesis.*)

In the course of that trip to Paran, the Israelites grew impatient with the manna and longed for some variety in the food. Once again, Moses turned to God for help. God reassured him and Moses passed the message on to the seventy elders of the people. When that happened:

> Num.11:25. . . . *the Lord . . . took of the spirit . . . and gave it unto the seventy elders: and . . . when the spirit rested upon them, they prophesied, and did not cease.*

I explained in *Words in Genesis* that the word "prophet" is derived from Greek words meaning "to speak for," so that a prophet is an interpreter. The great prophets of the Bible were interpreters of God's will and since God, according to the Biblical account, often chose to reveal the future through them, "prophet" has come to mean someone who can foretell the future.

However, there are many ways in which people

may believe that the will of a divine being is showing itself. In early times, when a person had hallucinations or was out of his head so that he acted in odd ways, it seemed to the onlookers that he must be under the control of some god or demon. The Israelites felt this, too, and they believed that a person who, in the course of deep religious emotion, fell to the ground and spoke or cried out incoherently was doing so under the influence of the Spirit of God. He was, therefore, prophesying.

A person prophesying in this manner is sometimes said to be in "ecstasy." Ecstasy is from Greek words meaning "out of his place" (or, as we would say today, "out of his right mind").

Strong emotion that does not involve religion may also make you seem out of your right mind for a while. Thus, you may stammer incoherently and choke or act senselessly when you are overcome with great rage, great fear, or great happiness. For some reason, "ecstasy" has come to be applied to great happiness in particular.

The Israelites obtained their change in diet in the form of quail, which swarmed over the camp. But then new trouble arose within Moses' own family. His sister and brother grew discontented:

Num.12:1. *And Miriam and Aaron spake*

*against Moses because of the Ethiopian woman whom he had married . . .*

"Ethiopian" is a word of Greek origin, used in place of the Hebrew word *Kushi.* In the Revised Standard Version, the woman whom Moses married is described as "Cushite."

A Cushite woman is a woman from the land of Cush. It has usually been assumed that Cush is the land we now call Ethiopia. However, there seems some reason to think that districts in southern Arabia were also known as Cush to the Israelites, so the woman may have been of an Arabian tribe. In fact, the verse may even refer to Moses' wife Zipporah, who was a Midianite and therefore Arabian. As a non-Israelite and a foreigner, she was resented by Miriam and Aaron, who used her as a device to rouse the people against Moses.

"Ethiopian" is from a Greek word meaning "burnt faces," in reference to the dark complexions of the African people living south of Egypt. In early modern times it came to be applied to Negroes (though the ruling classes of Ethiopia speak a Semitic language and do not consider themselves Negroes). It is on account of this verse, then, that Moses is often said to have married a Negro woman.

Having raised this emotional issue, Miriam and

Aaron went on to maintain that they themselves were just as qualified to appear as God's spokesman as Moses was. To this, Moses made no direct reply, perhaps because he hesitated to quarrel with his brother and sister. The Bible comments on this silence of his:

> Num.12:3. (*Now the man Moses was very meek, above all the men which were upon the face of the earth.*)

To be meek is to be mild of temper, patient under injuries. Now Moses, according to the Biblical accounts, was not particularly mild of temper. However, on this occasion he was, and, because of this verse, the expression "meek as Moses" has become a common way of saying "very meek."

With the Israelites in Paran, not far from the southern tip of Canaan, it was time to think about actually entering and conquering the land that had been promised to them.

Twelve men were therefore sent ahead into Canaan in order to bring back a report of the land and the state of its defenses. One man was taken from each tribe and, of them, only two are of any importance in later passages of the Bible. One is Joshua, of the tribe of Ephraim, who has already appeared as the military leader of the Israelites in the battle against the Amalekites and as Moses' minister on the slopes of Mount Sinai.

The other:

> Num.13:6. *Of the tribe of Judah, Caleb . . .*

Caleb's part in the story that is to follow is good enough to cause the name to be used in modern times. Caleb Cushing, for instance, was a nineteenth-century American statesman who was Attorney-General under President Franklin Pierce.

Moses gave the men their instructions:

> Num.13:17. . . . *Get you up this way southward and go up into the mountain.*

It seems strange to say "Get you up this way southward" when the Israelites were encamped to the south of Canaan and the twelve scouts would have to travel northward.

What Moses was actually saying, as expressed in the Revised Standard Version was, "Go up into the Negeb yonder."

The Negeb was that region of Canaan that lay between the Dead Sea and Paran. It occupied the southern stretches of what was later to become the Land of Israel.

To the Israelites, almost all of whom dwelt in the more fertile areas west and north of the Dead Sea, the dry area south of the Dead Sea was "the South," which is what "Negeb" means. The Biblical account used the word "Negeb" since that was the name of the area and it is possible to say "Go north to the South." Thus, a person on a ship in the Gulf of Mexico would have to steam northward to reach the American South.

By the phrase "go up into the mountain," by the way, is meant "travel through the highlands." The land of Israel consists of a coastal plain along the Mediterranean (controlled in the time of Moses, and for some centuries afterward, by the Philistines) and a rugged, hilly section between this plain and the Jordan Valley. This rugged section is often referred to as the "hill country."

The twelve followed instructions:

> Num.13:21. *So they went up, and searched the land from the wilderness of Zin unto Rehob . . .*
>
> Num.13:22. *And they . . . came unto Hebron; where Ahiman, Sheshai, and Talmai, the children of Anak, were. . . .*

The wilderness of Zin is part of the Negeb and represents the far south of Canaan. Rehob (ree′hob) is a place in the far north of Canaan. To search the land from Zin to Rehob meant, in other words, to investigate it from end to end.

The children of Anak (ay′nak) represent some early tribe of Canaanites who greatly impressed the scouts with their strength. This is not surprising since the early Canaanites, living in a territory that lay between the great civilizations of Egypt and Babylonia, had developed a considerable civilization of their own. They had built strong walled cities and had armies that were well trained and well armed. To the Israelites approaching from the desert, fresh from slavery, and without a warlike tradition, such cities and armies must have been a very disheartening sight.

The scouts brought back samples of the agricultural products of the land and all agreed that it was a fertile and desirable place to live in. However, most felt pretty discouraged about the strength of the Canaanites.

Caleb was all for an immediate attack but he was voted down. In fact, the pessimists among the scouts exaggerated the strength of the inhabitants by speaking of them as giants:

> Num.13:33. *And there we saw the giants, the sons of Anak . . . and we were in our own sight as grasshoppers . . .*

This may have been meant symbolically. The sons of Anak were giants in military strength, and in comparison with them, the scouts felt as weak as grasshoppers. However, in later times, the verse was taken literally. The sons of Anak were assumed to be so large that an ordinary man was no larger than a grasshopper in comparison. For that reason, "son of Anak" has come to be used as an expression meaning a huge giant.

At this report, the Israelites rebelled and refused to go any farther. In fact, they suggested the selection of new leaders who would take them back to Egypt.

Joshua and Caleb fought against this:

> Num.14:6. *And Joshua . . . and Caleb . . . which were of them that searched the land, rent their clothes:*

"Rend" ("rent" is the past tense) is a somewhat old-fashioned word for "tear apart." It was a customary sign of mourning among Israelites to tear their clothes, and it was also done when blasphemy was heard spoken. In this case, it was blasphemy for Israelites to suggest abandoning the land promised them by God and returning to the land from which God had taken them.

Joshua and Caleb tried to persuade the Israelites to

be of good courage, but they could not make themselves heard. At this, God, in anger, was ready to destroy the Israelites, but Moses persuaded Him to take lighter measures. God therefore condemned the Israelites to remain in the wilderness until all the adults who had been numbered in the census, but two, were dead. The two exceptions were, of course, Joshua and Caleb.

It would thus be the next generation, born in the wilderness and brought up to a hard life, with no memory of the fleshpots of Egypt, that would enter Canaan.

The ten scouts who had brought back a discouraging report died at once, and the Israelites, in despair, attempted to atone for their doubting by advancing at once in the direction of Canaan against Moses' advice. However, the Amalekites and other tribes met and defeated them.

At this point there is an interruption in the Biblical account during which further instructions are given with regard to sacrifices. In addition, there is a small incident concerning a Sabbath-breaker:

> Num.15:32. *And while the children of Israel were in the wilderness, they found a man that gathered sticks upon the sabbath day.*

He was taken before Moses and Aaron and was punishing by being stoned to death.

This story ends here as far as the Bible is concerned (except that it serves as a terrible example of what happens to someone who breaks the Sabbath). However, outside the Bible, it ends in the moon!

The moon, as we now know, has a rough and mountainous surface for the most part, but there are areas that are comparatively smooth and dark. The moon is close enough to the earth for these areas to show up as vague splotches. Without a telescope to show them clearly for what they are, men are free to imagine all sorts of explanations for the markings.

A great many different people seem to be able to make out the figure of a man in those dark areas and from this arose the phrase "the man in the moon."

In medieval Europe, the legend arose that the man in the moon was the particular man who was caught in the act of gathering sticks upon the Sabbath day. For that reason, he was pictured as carrying a bundle of sticks, or a thornbush. Later on, a dog was added (perhaps to let him have company).

In Shakespeare's play "*A Midsummer Night's Dream*, a play within a play is put on by laborers, and one of the characters is supposed to represent moonshine. He appears with a thornbush and a dog

— harking back to this verse, although there is nothing in either the Bible or in Jewish legend to place the Sabbath-breaker on the moon.

And now Moses found he had to face another rebellion, or rather a pair of them which the Bible seems to squeeze together to form one. Certain leaders of the tribe of Reuben, including two called Dathan and Abiram, maintained that Moses was making himself too powerful and that he had failed in his promise to bring them to Canaan. This was a political rebellion.

Again, a Levite called Korah, at the head of a number of men, objected to the fact that only Aaron and his descendants might be priests. They maintained that all Levites were equally holy.

Punishment was swift, however. With reference to the rebels:

> Num.16:32. *And the earth opened her mouth, and swallowed them up, and their houses and all the men . . .*
>
> Num.16:33. *They . . . went down alive into the pit, and the earth closed upon them: . . .*

The "pit" refers to the underground kingdom of the dead, called "Sheol" by the Jews, "Hades" by the Greeks, and "Hell" in English (I discuss these words in *Words in Genesis*). People dislike naming such a horrible place so they find other words for the purpose. "Pit" is one of them — just a hole in the ground. However, because of this verse, "pit" has become horrible, too. People speak with a shudder of "the pit of Hell," or "the bottomless Pit," or, sometimes, simply "the Pit."

As a further proof that Aaron's descendants alone were to be given the priestly office, each tribe was ordered to place a rod before the tabernacle, and Aaron was to place his rod among them. The result is described:

> Num.17:8. . . . *and, behold, the rod of Aaron . . . brought forth buds, and bloomed blossoms, and yielded almonds.*

For this reason, the term "Aaron's rod" has been given to a number of plants which are marked by a straight, tall stem upon which flowers grow. The goldenrod is an example.

But the long stay in the wilderness was drawing to a close and the generation that had fled from Egypt was dwindling. Even the family that led them was approaching its end:

Num.20:1. . . . *the people abode in Kadesh; and Miriam died there, and was buried there.*

Kadesh was the town that served as the Israelite base during the years in that part of the wilderness. It was between Paran and Zin, at the southern border of Canaan.

Then, when the Israelites suffered from lack of water, Moses and Aaron drew water from a rock, but in doing so, they displeased God in some manner. (The Bible is not clear and scholars are uncertain as to what actually took place.) As a result, it was decreed that neither Moses nor Aaron would be allowed to enter Canaan.

And now, at last, it was time to renew the drive against Canaan.

# 8

## Balaam

THE DIRECT APPROACH through the Negeb was not attempted. Instead, the decision was made to outflank the Canaanites. The Israelites would head eastward, circle the Dead Sea, and approach central Canaan from the east. In order to do that, some arrangement had to be made with the people who ruled the area that the Israelites would have to cross.

> Num.20:14. *And Moses sent messengers from Kadesh unto the king of Edom . . .*
>
> Num.20:17. *Let us pass, I pray thee, through thy country . . .*

Edom was the country lying south and southeast of the Dead Sea. It refused to allow passage to the Israelites although Moses guaranteed the absolute safety of the Edomites and their property. (Perhaps the Edomites were not sure that Moses could control every member of so large an army and, considering how often the Israelites had rebelled in the wilderness, perhaps he could not.)

However, this started over a thousand years of enmity between the Israelites and the Edomites. This enmity is traced back three centuries before Moses' time, in the Bible, to the rivalry of the twin brothers Jacob and Esau, the former being the ancestor of the Israelites, and the latter of the Edomites. (See *Words in Genesis.*)

As a result of Edom's refusal to allow passage and the making ready of her army to fight if necessary, the Israelites were forced to march around Edomite territory. This meant a doubling back toward the Gulf of Akaba again.

In doing so, they reached Mount Hor, which, according to tradition, is located halfway between the Dead Sea and the Gulf of Akaba. There Aaron died and his oldest remaining son, Eleazar, became the new high priest.

As a result of this, the Arabs call the mountain which is traditionally supposed to be the one on which Aaron died *Jebel Harun* ("Mount of Aaron").

After an appropriate period of mourning, the Israelites continued their march around Edom and then north. In this way, they passed to the east of Edom and to the east of the kingdom north of it:

> Num.21:11. *And they journeyed . . . in the wilderness which is before Moab, toward the sunrising. . . .*
>
> Num.21:13. *From thence they removed . . . on the other side of Arnon . . . for Arnon is the border of Moab, between Moab and the Amorites.*

To the north of Edom and directly east of the southern half of the Dead Sea lay the land of Moab. The Israelites traced the ancestry of the Moabites from Lot, the nephew of Abraham. It was a small country, only a little larger than the state of Rhode Island.

The Arnon River, which marked the northern

boundary of Moab, flows due west into the Dead Sea about halfway between the northern and southern limits of that salt lake. Its Arabic name today is *Wadi Mojib* ("River of Moab").

North of Moab was Amorite territory which Sihon, the Amorite king, had recently conquered from Moab.

Once again, Moses attempted to get permission for peaceful passage westward toward Canaan, this time from the Amorites. Like the Edomites, the Amorites refused, but now the Israelites had no choice. There was no way of getting around the Amorite territory, so an attack was necessary:

> Num.21:24. *And Israel smote him with the edge of the sword, and possessed his land from Arnon unto Jabbok, even unto the children of Ammon . . .*

The Jabbok River flows westward about forty miles north of the Arnon. It enters the Jordan River north of the Dead Sea. North of the Jabbok is the land of the Ammonites, whom the Israelites viewed as being descended, like the Moabites, from Lot.

The Amorite capital, Heshbon, is taken and occupied and the Bible then points out that this city is mentioned in an old Amorite victory song over

Moab. (Apparently, in later centuries, the song was still known, but the city had long since been destroyed and forgotten.) Part of the song goes:

> Num.21:29. *Woe to thee, Moab! Thou art undone, O people of Chemosh . . .*

Chemosh (kee′mosh) was the god of the Moabites and, in later centuries, it was to be one of the surrounding gods whose worship sometimes gained popularity in the land of Israel. In later times, all these neighboring gods were viewed as members of the band of fallen angels of whom the Book of Enoch spoke. Chemosh is one of the band of angels who in the first part of Milton's *Paradise Lost* are pictured as having been hurled down into hell by the victorious angels that were loyal to God.

After the defeat of the Amorites, the Israelite armies carried out raids to the far north:

> Num.21:33. *And they turned and went up by the way of Bashan: and Og the king of Bashan went out against them . . .*
>
> Num.21:35. *So they smote him . . . and they possessed his land.*

Bashan (bay′shun) is a territory north of the Ammonite lands and to the east of the lake that was later called the Sea of Galilee. It was a fertile land and was undoubtedly a valuable source of food for the Israelite army.

The Israelite army was now established on the eastern boundary of Canaan:

> Num.22:1. *And the children of Israel . . . pitched . . . on this side Jordan . . .*

They were on the east of the river, and on the west was Canaan. The Jordan River rises in what is now the borderland between Lebanon and Syria and flows southward to the Sea of Galilee and farther south to the Dead Sea. It is 200 miles long, winding and not navigable. Much of it is below sea level because it is set in a deep valley that marks the northernmost end of a rift in the earth's crust that extends all the way down to east-central Africa.

Some think the word "Jordan" comes from a Hebrew word meaning "to descend," because the hill country to the west drops steeply toward the Jordan and the Dead Sea, or perhaps because the river level itself drops rapidly on its passage to the low-lying Dead Sea. (The surface of the Dead Sea is 1286 feet below sea level.)

The Jordan, because of its connection with Biblical events, is probably the most famous small river in the world. It formed the eastern boundary of Canaan in the time of Moses and it formed the eastern boundary of Palestine after World War I. In 1921, when the British took the area from the Turks, they organized the territory east of the Jordan River as "Transjordania," meaning "across the Jordan." Later, the name was shortened to "Transjordan."

Transjordan included most of the territory conquered by the Israelites under Moses. It included the territories that in Moses' time belonged to the Moabites, the Amorites, and the Ammonites. The capital city of Transjordan was in what had once been Ammonite territory and its name is "Amman" even now, a clear reminder of Canaanite days.

In 1949, after the modern state of Israel had been established, Transjordan annexed some of the Arabic-speaking portions west of the Jordan River and was no longer entirely "across" it. The name of the country was then changed to "Jordan."

By now, with the Israelite army on the banks of the Jordan, Balak (bay′lak), king of Moab, was in a panic. He might not have minded the Israelites attacking and defeating the Amorites, who were enemies of Moab, and perhaps that is why he didn't combine with the Amorites against the invaders. Now, however, with the Israelites located where the Amorites had been, the newcomers seemed even stronger and more dangerous than the old enemy.

Balak did not dare meet the Israelites in open battle, so he decided on another course of action. He sent for a renowned wizard, Balaam (bay′lam), to curse the Israelites. In those days, such curses were considered very effective. Balaam seemed a particularly good choice because he is described as being a worshiper of Yahweh and therefore should be able to turn the Israelites' own God against them.

Balak sent high officials of his government:

> Num.22:7. *And the elders of Moab . . . departed with the rewards of divination in their hand; and they came unto Balaam . . .*

This makes it quite plain that Balaam worked for hire, and performed his blessings and curses for a fee. For that reason, the expression "Balaamite" is sometimes used for anyone who makes a profit out of religion.

Balaam was reluctant to go but, eventually, consented:

> Num.22:21. *And Balaam rose up in the morning, and saddled his ass, and went with the princes of Moab.*

In those days, the ass was the common animal used for ordinary riding. The horse was an extremely expensive animal that was used only for war-chariots.

The animal that is called "ass" throughout the Bible is better known to us as "donkey." Actually, "donkey" is a modern word that only entered the English language in the eighteenth century and its origin is uncertain. Some people actually think it comes from the first two syllables of "Don Quixote." This might be because Don Quixote's squire (in the great Spanish novel by Cervantes) had an ass named Dapple that played an important part in the story. Or else it might be that Don Quixote himself might seem to some people to have been an ass. (An ass is supposed to be stupid, which is why we use the word "asinine." It comes from the Latin *asinus*, meaning "ass." However, the ass is not stupid at all, and neither was Don Quixote, so perhaps the origin of "donkey" remains a mystery.)

In the case of Balaam, his ass proved wiser than he and, in a way of speaking, a greater wizard. God was angry at Balaam's leaving to curse Israel and stood in Balaam's path with a drawn sword. The ass saw the divine presence and three times tried to avoid it and was beaten for its pains.

> Num.22:28. *And the Lord opened the mouth of the ass, and she said unto Balaam, What have I done unto thee, that thou hast smitten me these three times?*

It was then made possible for Balaam to see the angel and recognize the danger he had been in. Balaam was allowed to continue but only on condition that he speak what God put in his mouth and not what Balak would expect him to say.

The story of Balaam's ass is, except for the serpent in the Garden of Eden (see *Words in Genesis*), the only case of a talking animal in the Bible. It was a kind of wonder story and, naturally, it attracted the attention of the readers of the Bible.

It was not the impressive sort of miracle like God's voice coming out of a burning bush, or the parting of the Red Sea. It was, instead, something almost humorous. This has its effect on the press. In newspapers, it is customary to keep in standing type little items about the odd or amazing to fill in any gaps in the columns that the legitimate news might leave. These are sometimes called "Balaams," apparently because they often concern matters as queer and bizarre as a talking donkey.

Eventually, Balaam reached Moab and was taken to a height overlooking the Israelite army. He then began what was supposed to be his curse:

> Num.23:7. *And he took up his parable, and said . . .*

This sounds as though he lifted a staff or some ritualistic object. Actually, "parable" comes from Greek words meaning "side by side" and is a translation of a Hebrew word meaning the same thing. The Hebrew form of poetry consisted, very frequently, of comparisons, in which a succession of ideas were stated in two different ways placed side by side, thus being subtly and cleverly compared. Balaam begins, for instance, by describing Balak's instructions and his own response:

> Num.23:7. . . . *Balak . . . brought me . . . saying, Come, curse me Jacob, and come, defy Israel.*
>
> Num.23:8. *How shall I curse, whom God has not cursed? or how shall I defy, whom the Lord hath not defied?*

Naturally, some of the beauty and power of this type of poetry is lost in the translation, though the writers of the Authorized Version managed miraculously well. Then, too, we ourselves are so used to poetry that involves a fixed rhythm of syllables, and usually a pattern of rhyme, that our unaccustomed ears miss the delight that a person brought up to the Hebrew language would find in this.

In any case, the word "parable" came to mean any form of expression that involved this poetry of comparison. Oracular statements, such as those of Balaam, usually appeared as such poetry and were, therefore, parables. So you see, "to take up a parable" is merely to begin an oration.

In later times, the word "parable" took on a slightly different meaning and, to avoid confusion, the Revised Standard Version drops the word in this book. It has chapter 23, verse 7 of the Book of Numbers begin, "And Balaam took up his discourse . . ."

Balaam completes his oracle and it turns out to be a blessing, rather than a curse. The disappointed Balak takes him to a second height, hoping that the new ground may be a better one for cursing.

Balaam repeats a second oracle and once again it is a blessing. In the course of it he says:

> Num.23:22. *God brought them out of Egypt; he hath as it were the strength of an unicorn.*

The Hebrew word which is here translated "unicorn" is *re'em.* Most scholars consider this word to mean the wild ox (now extinct), which is the ancestor of modern cattle. In fact, the Revised Standard Version has the verse read, "they have as it were the horns of the wild ox."

However, when the Bible was translated into Greek, the word *re'em* was somehow translated into *monokeros* (meaning "one-horn") and in Latin this became *unicornis* (still meaning "one-horn").

Why this should be is uncertain. One theory, which sounds plausible, is that the Assyrians constructed large reliefs of wild oxen which were shown in profile so that one horn covered the second. The Greeks, coming across such sculptured forms in later centuries, without personal knowledge of the wild ox might have thought it had only one horn in reality and called it by that name.

In the Middle Ages, the mythmakers elaborated on the theme of the unicorn and began to imagine it as a horselike creature with one long, tightly twisted horn growing out of the middle of its forehead. There is, indeed, a kind of whale (the narwhal) which has one tooth that grows out of its jaw as a long, twisted object. Pieces of it might have been brought back by sailors who claimed it to be the horn of the unicorn in order to sell it for large sums, since a unicorn horn was supposed to have magical properties.

As the Middle Ages wore to a close, attempts on the part of naturalists to deny that the unicorn existed were opposed by some religious leaders who felt that the unicorn must exist because it was mentioned in the Bible. But, of course, it was not. It was the wild ox that was mentioned and the unicorn is only a creature of mistake and mistranslation.

Balaam next goes on to praise the Israelites extravagantly:

> Num:23:23. *Surely there is no enchantment against Jacob, neither is there any divination against Israel: according to this time it shall be said of Jacob and of Israel, What hath God wrought!*

This verse has had an interesting echo in the history of modern science. In the 1830's, the American physicist Joseph Henry devised an electric relay and showed how it could be used to transmit messages across long distances at the speed of light. An American artist named Samuel F. B. Morse was interested in working out such a "telegraph" (from Greek words meaning "far-writing"). In this, he had Henry's help. By 1844, Morse had gouged an appropriation of money out of Congress and had strung wires the forty-mile distance from Baltimore to Washington.

And the first message sent over this first telegraph was "What hath God wrought!" — the words of Balaam.

Balaam's second oracle proved a better blessing than the first, and therefore even worse than the first from the standpoint of Moab. Nevertheless, Balak decided to try one last time. He took Balaam to still another hilltop, and the wizard began a third oracle.

This third oracle, however, was still a blessing and Balak, in anger, sent Balaam away. Balaam explained that he could only repeat the words God put in his mouth and in a fourth oracle, foretold the future:

> Num.24:17. . . . *there shall come a Star out of Jacob, and a Sceptre shall rise out of Israel, and shall smite the corners of Moab, and destroy all the children of Sheth.*

The word "Sheth" looks as though it is a proper name, but it is a Hebrew word which means "tumult" or possibly "pride," so that "children of Sheth" may mean something as ordinary as "troublemakers."

The "Star" and the "Sceptre" are poetic references to a ruler of Israel. In later times, David, the greatest of Israel's kings, did indeed conquer Moab so that one might suppose the words refer to him.

However, after the destruction of the Hebrew kingdoms, it may have been felt that this verse could not refer to David since his work was later undone. It must refer then to some future king who would conquer the "troublemakers" permanently.

To many Christians it seems the reference must be to Jesus. To indicate that, the words "Star" and

"Sceptre" are capitalized in the Authorized Version, as words referring to God or to Jesus usually are in the English language. In the Revised Standard Version, however, the words are not capitalized.

After further comments which are today a little obscure in some cases, Balaam went his way at last, and Balak had had no good of him after all.

And now as the actual battle for Canaan was soon to begin, it was time for a second census to check on the numbers of fighting men. The first census had taken place thirty-eight years earlier at Sinai, under the supervision of Moses and Aaron. This one was under the supervision of Moses and Eleazar. The results are given as follows:

| | | |
|---|---|---|
| Reuben | 43,730 | (a loss of 2,770) |
| Simeon | 22,200 | (a loss of 37,100) |
| Gad | 40,500 | (a loss of 5,150) |
| Judah | 76,500 | (a gain of 1,900) |
| Issachar | 64,300 | (a gain of 9,900) |
| Zebulun | 60,500 | (a gain of 3,100) |
| Manasseh | 52,700 | (a gain of 20,500) |
| Ephraim | 32,500 | (a loss of 8,000) |
| Benjamin | 45,600 | (a gain of 10,200) |
| Dan | 64,400 | (a gain of 1,700) |
| Asher | 53,400 | (a gain of 11,900) |
| Naphtali | 45,400 | (a loss of 8,000) |
| TOTAL | 601,730 | (a loss of 1,820) |

The greatest change in numbers was the case of Simeon, which was now the smallest of the twelve tribes (excluding Levi).

Another purpose of the census was to determine how large a share of Canaan each tribe was to receive. (For that reason, some details as to different clans within each tribe were given in reporting the second census.)

However, the Israelites already possessed land to the east of the Jordan, and some of the tribes, including Reuben and Gad and a few of the clans of Manasseh, asked for allotments out of that territory. They promised to fight in Canaan with the remaining tribes and to return to the allotted land only after Canaan was conquered.

Moses approved:

> Num.32:40. *And Moses gave Gilead unto Machir the son of Manasseh; and he dwelt therein.*

According to the Biblical account, as given during the second census, Machir (may'ker) was the only son of Manasseh. For that reason, "Machir" was often used as an alternate name for the tribe of Manasseh, particularly in poetic writing.

Furthermore, a son of Machir is recorded as Gilead, so that the land of Gilead, on which the clans of

Manasseh settled, derives its name from their ancestor. This sort of naming is common among ancient peoples, as I explained in *Words in Genesis*.

There is then a final summary of the various places of encampment during the forty years in the wilderness from the time of the Exodus to the time when the Israelites reached the Jordan River. This and a few more regulations concerning the division of Canaan and the inheritance of land brings the Book of Numbers to an end.

# 9

## Jordan

THE FIFTH BOOK of the Bible, the last of the Pentateuch, takes place on the eastern banks of the Jordan as the Israelites wait for the signal to cross. It consists of speeches made by Moses for the purpose of summing up, for the Israelites, all that had happened since they had left Egypt, and to go over, once again, the Law.

Since the book contains a repetition of some of the Law and, in particular, of the Ten Commandments, the Greek name of the book is a good one. This is *Deuteronomy* (dyoo′ter-on′oh-mee, "second law-giving"). Actually, however, although it is a good name, it arose out of a mistranslation, which I shall mention later.

I shall use "Deut." as its abbreviation.

The Hebrew name, as you might expect, is taken from the first line:

> Deut.1:1. *These be the words which Moses spake . . .*

The Hebrew name for the book is *elleh hadevarim* ("these be the words"), or simply *devarim* ("words").

Moses' first oration reviews the events that took place during the march from Sinai (which is called by its alternate name, Horeb, here) to Canaan. He begins with God's instructions to take Canaan:

> Deut.1:7. *Turn you . . . to the mount of the Amorites, and unto all the places nigh thereunto . . . and unto Lebanon . . .*

Lebanon represents here part of the northern limit of the land to be settled by the Israelites. It is the section of Mediterranean seacoast north of the land of Israel. It received its name from the Hebrew word for "white," because of the snow-covered mountain ranges that run its length.

The mountain ranges are two in number, and in Greek and Roman times the western range, nearer the sea, was called "Libanus," while the eastern range was "Anti-Libanus" ("opposite the Libanus"). The lowland between the ranges is referred to as the "Valley of Lebanon" in the Bible. The Greeks called it "Coele-Syria" ("hollow Syria") because it was the part of Syria that lay in the hollow between the mountains.

In modern times, the region of Lebanon was Turkish until after World War I. In 1920, it was put under French trusteeship, but in 1944, it was granted its independence, and its name is once more on the map.

Moses next describes the march and the victories won by the Israelites. He gives some details about Og of Bashan that were not given in the Book of Numbers:

> Deut.3:11. *For only Og king of Bashan remained of the remnant of giants; behold, his bedstead was . . . of iron; . . . nine cubits was*

*the length thereof, and four cubits the breadth of it.*

The bedstead would seem to be the iron frame supporting Og's bed, if we take it at face value. Some scholars consider "bedstead" to refer to his coffin or sarcophagus. In any case, counting 18 inches to the cubit, the bedstead was 13½ feet long and 6 feet wide. This is pretty large and any man who could fill it or nearly fill it, whether it was a bedframe or a coffin, would be considered a giant.

Later legends, however, made Og much larger than that. He was supposed to be mountainously high and to have lived from before the time of Noah's Flood. Concerning that time, the Book of Genesis (6:4) says: "There were giants in the earth in those days . . ." Tales were told how Og survived the Flood by straddling the ark.

Then in the war with Moses, at which time he was supposedly 5000 years old, he was pictured as having heaved a mountain up from its roots to throw at the Israelites, but Moses himself quickly struck him with a blow of the sword and the giant bled to death.

None of these extravagant stories are in the Bible, of course, but Og of Bashan has remained, ever since, one of the great giants of legend. In later books of the Bible, the defeat of Og is looked back upon as one of the great blessings conferred upon Israel by God.

And, having completed the short run-through of the wanderings through the wilderness, Moses urged the Israelites to remain faithful to the worship of God and to the commandments given them.

In Moses' second address he gives a summary of the Law. He begins by repeating the Ten Commandments. Then he addresses an impassioned plea that the Israelites never forget the Law:

> Deut.6:4. *Hear, O Israel: The Lord our God is one Lord.*

This is the fundamental creed of Judaism, and is the most revered single verse of the Bible to Jews. It is referred to as the "Shema" ("Hear") from its first word.

Moses then goes on to say:

> Deut.6:5. *And thou shalt love the Lord thy God with all thine heart, and with all thy soul, and with all thy might.*
>
> Deut.6:6. *And these words, which I command thee this day, shall be in thine heart:*
>
> Deut.6:7. *And thou shalt teach them diligently unto thy children . . .*

Deut.6:8. *And thou shalt bind them for a sign upon thine hand, and they shall be as frontlets between thine eyes.*

Deut.6:9. *And thou shalt write them upon the posts of thy house, and on thy gates.*

These verses could be taken symbolically. Binding the law on the hand and about the brow (a "frontlet" is a band about the brow, designed to keep the hair in place) might mean that the hand should always act according to the Law and the mind should always think according to the Law.

Later Jews, about the first century B.C., however, began to interpret these verses literally. It was impractical to wear the entire Law on hands and brows, but they wrote the passage quoted above, together with other similar passages, including also the Shema and enclosed them in leather pouches attached to long leather straps. One pouch could be bound about the arm and another about the forehead. In Hebrew, these were called *tephillin*, meaning "prayer bands." As time passed, a complicated ritual was developed which dictated exactly how the leather straps were to be wound, what prayers were to be said, and so on.

In addition, Biblical passages, including the Shema, were placed in little tubes of wood or metal, which were then attached to the entranceway into a dwelling place. This was meant to follow the instructions of chapter 6, verse 9 of the Book of Deuteronomy. Such a tube on the side of the door may be seen at the entrance to the house or apartment of many Jews even today. The tube is called a *mezuzah,* which is Hebrew for "doorpost."

Both "tephillin" and "mezuzah" are to be found in Webster's Unabridged Dictionary and have therefore become part of the vast vocabulary of the English language. However, a much more familiar term, for "tephillin" at least, is "phylactery" (fih-lak′ter-ee), which is derived from Greek words meaning "a guard." This could be interpreted to mean that the phylacteries guarded the man who wore them against forgetfulness of the Law.

Moses further goes on to say:

> Deut.6:16. *Ye shall not tempt the Lord your God . . .*

This is a famous verse, because, for one thing, it was quoted by Jesus in the New Testament. However, the use of an old-fashioned word obscures the meaning of the verse. To us nowadays, "tempt" means "to lure into evil." An older meaning, as I explained in *Words in Genesis,* is "to test" or "to put to trial."

Clearly, it would not be proper for a man to put

God to the test and to say, for instance, "If God exists, let him prove it by doing thus and so." God, in the view of the Biblical writers, was not a being to be made to do something at the command of a man.

The Revised Standard Version makes this clear by having the verse read, "You shall not put the Lord your God to the test . . ."

A little later, in speaking of the manna, Moses makes use of another phrase which has become a proverbial expression partly because Jesus quoted this, too:

> Deut.8:3. . . . *man doth not live by bread only, but by every word that proceedeth out of the mouth of the Lord doth man live.*

The meaning is that man's soul must be nourished as well as his body.

Moses goes on to recount those times in the wilderness when the Israelites rebelled, stressing how ungrateful they were to God. He goes on to speak of the importance of not being ungrateful in the future, and of destroying all forms of idolatry in Canaan after its conquest, and of resisting any impulse to worship other gods. He warns against men who might lure others away to the worship of false gods:

Deut.13:13. *Certain men, the children of Belial, are . . . saying, Let us go and serve other gods . . .*

In this verse (and in other verses in the Bible which mention "daughter of Belial," "man of Belial," and so on) it seems as though "Belial" (bee′lee-ul) is a proper name, especially since it is capitalized, and perhaps the name of a devil. Actually, this is not so. "Belial" is a Hebrew word meaning "unprofitable" or "worthless." A "child of Belial" or a "man of Belial" is a "worthless person." He is someone who understands so little that by listening to him you can gain no profit, nothing of worth.

The Revised Standard Version makes the verse begin, "Certain base fellows . . ."

Just the same, the existence of this verse and others like it caused many people to accept "Belial" as the name of a devil. It is mentioned in this way in the New Testament, for instance, and, in *Paradise Lost*, Milton has "Belial" as the name of one of the fallen angels.

Moses then goes on to repeat the dietary laws, the rules governing the treatment of servants, and the rules concerning the keeping of the various festivals. The manner of making judgments is described and even the rules to follow in choosing a king, when that became necessary. The future king is instructed that he, too, is subject to the Law:

> Deut.17:18. *And it shall be, when he sitteth upon the throne of his kingdom, that he shall write him a copy of this law . . .*
>
> Deut.17:19. *And it shall be with him, and he shall read therein all the days of his life . . .*
>
> Deut.17:20. *That his heart be not lifted up above his brethren . . .*

The phrase in Deut. 17:18, given in the Authorized Version as "a copy of this law," was incorrectly translated into Greek by the Alexandrian Jews, as *deuteronomion*, meaning "a second law." The mistake seems a natural one. A "copy of the law" is indeed a "second law" since now two written documents exist. However, to say "second law" implies a difference from the first one, while to say "a copy of the law" implies a version that is identical with the first one.

Nevertheless, it is from the mistaken word *deuteronomion* that the name of the Book of Deuteronomy arises.

There is also once more a warning against witchcraft:

> Deut.18:10. *There shall not be found among you . . . an observer of times . . .*
>
> Deut.18:11. *. . . or a necromancer.*

Other varieties of "wise men" are mentioned, but I choose these two because they have not been mentioned previously. An "observer of times" would be one who observes the changing positions of the planets from day to day — what we would call, today, an "astrologer." The Revised Standard Version uses instead the words "soothsayer" and "augur."

A soothsayer is one who "says sooth," "sooth" being an archaic word meaning "truth." He tells the truth about the future through his skill with divining. The word "augur" comes from the Latin word for "bird." One of the chief methods of divining the future was to note the flight of birds, the direction, the number, the kind, and so on.

The chief diviners of Rome were called "augurs" and the appearance of birds was "auspice" ("bird-sight"). Any number of English words are derived from these. We still say something "augurs well" or is "auspicious" when we mean that the future looks pleasant. Officials were inducted into office only when the omens were favorable, and so the President of the United States is still "inaugurated." "Augustus" is a good-luck name, meaning "of favorable auguries," so the first Roman emperor took it, giving us the adjective "august" and the name of the month "August," and a number of proper names both male and female—"Augustine," "Austin," and "Augusta," for instance.

As for "necromancer," that is from Latin words meaning "divining from dead bodies," because diviners would consult the spirits of the dead, and also study the internal organs of dead animals.

A discussion of the role of the Levites follows, and of prophets, both true and false:

> Deut.18:15. *The Lord thy God will raise up unto thee a Prophet from the midst of thee . . . unto him ye shall hearken . . .*

To many Christians, this verse seems to be a prediction of the coming of Jesus. It is for this reason that the word "prophet" is capitalized in the Authorized Version. It is not capitalized in the Revised Standard Version.

The word "hearken," by the way, is an old-fashioned word for "listen to." It gives rise to the exclamation "hark!" meaning "listen." The word "to hear" comes from the same root as "hearken"; it is the first syllable of the word.

Many chapters are then given over to a restatement of other laws, followed by a series of rather fearful curses upon the Israelites if they fail to follow God's commandments.

After a short third speech, Moses, at God's instruction, writes a song intended to serve as a perpetual reminder to the Israelites of future generations of the goodness of God and the sin of ingratitude.

God is described at the beginning of the poem:

> Deut.32:4. *He is the Rock, his work is perfect: for all his ways are judgment: a God of truth and without iniquity, just and right is he.*

It is common to use a rock to symbolize something secure and firm and unchangeable, something that will protect without flinching. In this case it is used to symbolize God and is therefore capitalized.

This same metaphor is used in some hymns, of which by far the most famous is one called "The Rock of Ages," written by an English clergyman named Augustus Montague Toplady, in 1775. Since God is eternal, he is a rock not only for now, but for all ages.

The love of God for Israel is described:

> Deut.32:10. . . . *he led him about, he instructed him, he kept him as the apple of his eye.*

The "apple of the eye" is not an actual apple, merely something that is small and round like an apple; in other words, the pupil. Since it is through the pupil that light enters the eye, the pupil is the most precious visible part of the organ we all cherish. Because of this verse, the "apple of your eye" has become a common phrase to describe something that is very dear to you.

And yet Israel, once it was made prosperous by God, rebelled:

> Deut.32:15. *But Jeshurun waxed fat, and kicked . . .*

Jeshurun means "the upright one" and it is used in Hebrew poetry, sometimes, to stand for the land and people of Israel; just as in our own poetry "Columbia" or "Land of Liberty" might stand for the United States.

Moses points out how inferior other forms of worship and other gods are:

> Deut.32:33. *Their wine is the poison of dragons . . .*

The word "dragon" is a translation of the Hebrew word *tannin,* which means simply "monster," and could represent any large and terrifying creature.

The Revised Standard Version has it: "Their wine is the poison of serpents."

We have come to think of a dragon as a particular kind of monster — a huge, flying lizard that breathes flame. Such a dragon is a matter of pure legend and has no relation to any "dragon" mentioned in the Authorized Version.

With the song concluded, Moses, as a last official act, blesses the various tribes; all that is, except Simeon. Actually, Simeon was a dying tribe. According to the account in the Book of Numbers, the population of the tribe of Simeon had declined by more than half during the stay in the wilderness. In the later books of the Bible, the tribe is not mentioned. It seems to have been absorbed by the tribe of Judah.

The tribe of Reuben did not flourish either. It is mentioned in the Book of Judges, for instance, but it performs no great feats. Before the time of David, it was absorbed by the neighboring tribe of Gad and by the alien Moabites. All that Moses, in his blessing, can give the tribe of Reuben is a brief statement hoping that it will not die out.

And now it is time for Moses to die:

> Deut: 34:1. *And Moses went up from the plains of Moab unto the mountain of Nebo, to the top of Pisgah . . . And the Lord shewed him all the land . . .*

> Deut.34:4. *And the Lord said . . . I have caused thee to see it with thine eyes, but thou shalt not go over thither.*

Mount Nebo (or Mount Pisgah, since the two names are used synonymously) is identified nowadays with a mountain about ten miles east of the northern end of the Dead Sea. Moses, in bringing the Israelites to the borders of Canaan, and seeing it from a mountaintop, but not entering it himself, remains a symbol of all men who don't quite live to see their labors reach a successful conclusion.

And then Moses died and was buried by God in a valley in Moab at a spot unknown to man. And the Bible's epitaph is:

> Deut.34:10. *And there arose not a prophet since in Israel like unto Moses . . .*

But history goes on, regardless of the death of individuals. With Moses gone, the leadership of the people of Israel passed to Joshua, and now a new phase of Israelite history was to open.

The Egyptian interlude of slavery was over. The struggles in the wilderness were past. The Law had been received.

Now it was time to enter Canaan, the Promised Land. . . .

## The House of Levi

Levi

Gershon Kohath Merari

Amram — Jochebed (f) Izhar Hebron Uzziel

Korah

Miriam (f) Aaron* — Elisheba (f) Moses — Zipporah (f)

Gershom

Nadab Abihu Eleazar* Ithamar

Phinehas*

*High Priests (f) Female

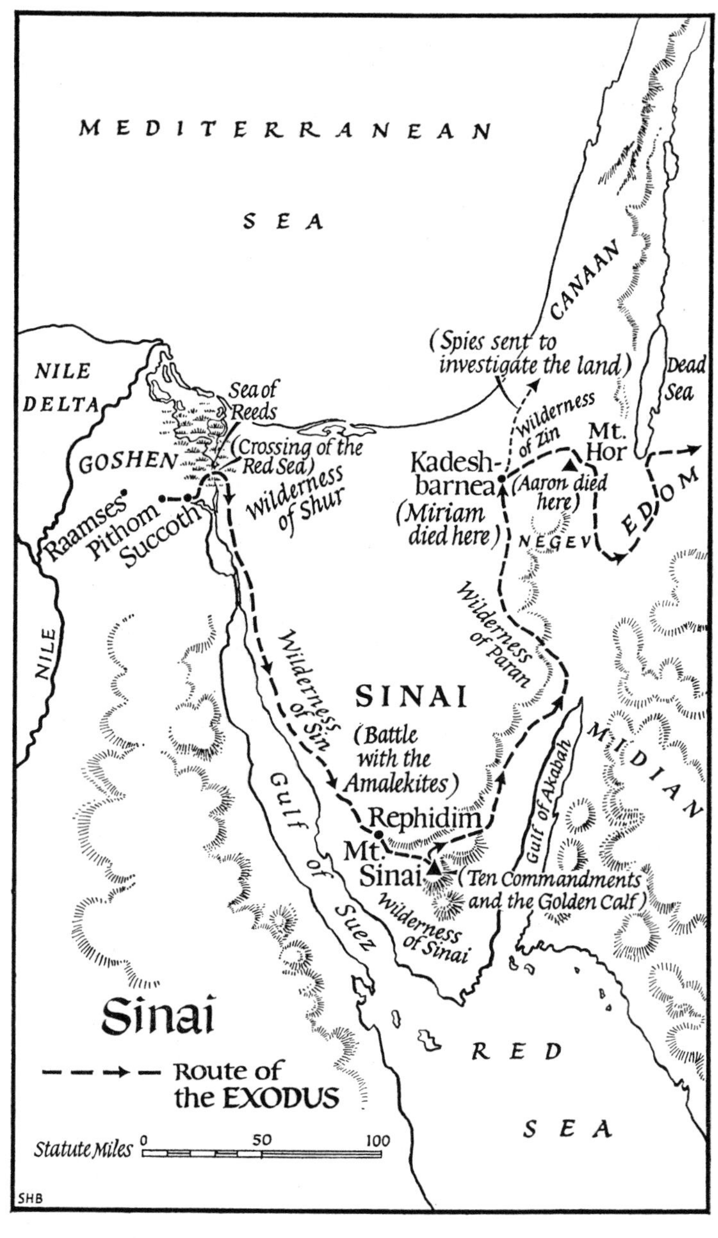
MEDITERRANEAN
SEA
CANAAN
(Spies sent to investigate the land)
Dead Sea
NILE DELTA
Sea of Reeds
(Crossing of the Red Sea)
GOSHEN
Raamses
Pithom
Succoth
Wilderness of Shur
Wilderness of Zin
Kadesh-barnea
Mt. Hor
(Aaron died here)
(Miriam died here)
NEGEV
EDOM
Wilderness of Paran
NILE
SINAI
Wilderness of Sin
(Battle with the Amalekites)
MIDIAN
Gulf of Akabah
Rephidim
Mt. Sinai
(Ten Commandments and the Golden Calf)
Gulf of Suez
Wilderness of Sinai
Sinai
Route of the EXODUS
RED SEA
Statute Miles 0 50 100
SHB

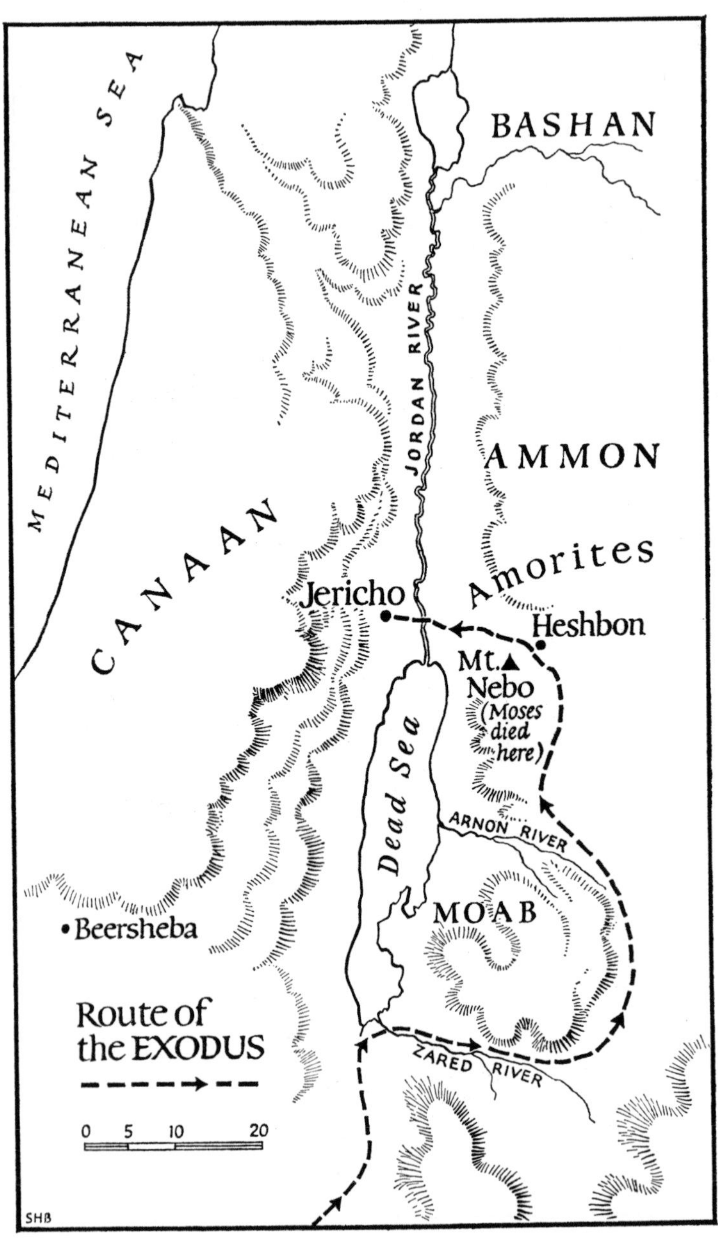
MEDITERRANEAN SEA
BASHAN
JORDAN RIVER
AMMON
CANAAN
Amorites
Jericho
Heshbon
Mt.
Nebo
(Moses
died
here)
Dead Sea
ARNON RIVER
MOAB
Beersheba
Route of
the EXODUS
0 5 10 20
ZARED RIVER
SHB

INDEX